when the dying speak

when the dying speak

how to listen to and learn from those facing death

RON WOOTEN-GREEN

LOYOLAPRESS.
A JESUIT MINISTRY
Chicago

LOYOLA PRESS.
A JESUIT MINISTRY

3441 N. Ashland Avenue
Chicago, Illinois 60657
(800) 621-1008
www.loyolapress.com

Interior design by Kathy Kikkert

Library of Congress Cataloging-in-Publication Data
Wooten-Green, Ronald.
    When the dying speak: how to listen to and learn from those facing death/Ronald
        Wooten-Green p.cm.
    Includes bibliographical references (p.).
    ISBN-13: 978-0-8294-1685-5; ISBN-10: 0-8294-1685-4
      1. Death—Religious aspects—Christianity. 2. Deathbed hallucinations. I Title.
    BT825.W65 2002
    248.8'66—dc21   2001050378

Printed in the United States of America
08 09 10 11 12 13 14 Bang 10 9 8 7 6 5 4 3

dedication

TO THE MEMORY OF DAWN ELIZABETH O'BRIEN GREEN, IN
GRATITUDE FOR THE WAY SHE SHARED
THE RICH DETAIL OF HER JOURNEY TO HER GOD
AND FOR INTRODUCING THIS SOJOURNER TO
A WHOLE NEW WORLD.

contents

~

foreword

On a busy Friday after two wedding rehearsals and a funeral service for a priest of the diocese, I walked over to a restaurant and, seated at the counter, ordered a hamburger and a chocolate milkshake. It was 9:00 p.m. I was hungry, fatigued, and mentally drained, but I dutifully opened this manuscript and began to flip halfheartedly through the pages. Beginning chapter one, I was immediately captivated by the author's description of his dying wife, Dawn, about the voices she heard, and about a heaven-bound bus she would soon board.

That brief sampling totally engaged me, and I found myself exclaiming, much to the surprise of my waiter: "This is a terrific book!"

The author is a remarkably gifted storyteller. From the description of Val, the earthy over-the-road truck driver who has a near death experience, to Carl, a man who feels compelled to reconcile with his son so they can "go around on the carousel" once more before his death, Ronald Wooten-Green mesmerizes the reader with these real-life accounts.

When the Dying Speak deals with a reality facing each one of us. This book offers examples, insights, and suggestions that will likely prove invaluable for many readers. The weekend after reading the manuscript, I used the story of Dawn and her heaven-bound bus at the conclusion of my homily. Our organist was struck by the story. His own wife had died several years ago after struggling with MS. "When Joan was dying," he said, "she had very similar experiences."

Sooner or later we must all come to grips with our own mortality. From adolescence through old age, we frequently deal with dying and death experiences. Every person does. Health care personnel, clergy, and people in the bereavement profession or ministry do so even more often and on a regular basis. Through these stories the author, a hospice chaplain, indirectly reveals his own admirable listening ability and extraordinary ministry skills. We can all learn from him.

Ron Wooten-Green has indeed written a terrific book, one that is real and on target, a volume that should enlighten and comfort many people. As he reminds us at the end of chapter five, "Listening to the Call of the Lord,"

Death is not the end.

Our loved one is not and will not be alone.

Moving from here to there is not frightening.

FATHER JOSEPH CHAMPLIN
RECTOR, CATHEDRAL OF THE
IMMACULATE CONCEPTION
SYRACUSE, NEW YORK 13202
OCTOBER 2001

acknowledgments

This book would not exist if it were not for
- Jim Radde, S.J. who urged this chaplain to "write the stories"
- Linda, who prodded her husband, believing in his ability to make the stories real and, like the artist she is, saw the diamond in the rubble
- Vinita Wright, who believed in the possibility and so sensitively edited it into reality
- The countless numbers of dying people and their families who trusted enough to share their stories
- The evening I sat on the edge of Dawn's bed thanking her for all that she had been able to share with me concerning her preparation for "catching the bus" to her God and her response: "Then you need to share it with others.

CHAPTER ONE

～

why it is so important
to listen to the dying

•

*i*t was late evening, and I had just finished getting my wife, Dawn, ready for the night. I wanted to get to bed because recent experience told me that this, too, would be an active night, with Dawn waking up and wanting to talk (not necessarily to me but to others in the room unseen by me). She seemed agitated, a sure sign that another night of sleep deprivation was in the offing.

"You seem upset, Dawn. What is it?"

"I just don't know how to get from here to there." Her tone was one of consternation.

"From here to where?" Even though I was sure I knew the answer, I thought I should ask. Without hesitation, this fifty-one-year-old woman, who now appeared as if she were at least eighty, said, "Well, heaven, of course!"

The next day when I came home for lunch, I walked into our bedroom to find Dawn sitting up in her bed amid a completely changed atmosphere. "You look so happy, Honey!" I said, suspecting that perhaps she had received a call from one of her siblings or one of our kids.

"Oh, Ron. Those people who have been hanging around here have given me a ticket for the bus and have invited me to go with them!" She beamed as if she had just won the world's greatest sweepstakes.

In a very real sense that is exactly what had happened. I hardly needed to ask about the destination of this bus. I knew that for those with a ticket, those with the vision to really see, the sign over the windshield of this bus would read *Heaven Bound*.

This book is written because of that bus. Dawn's ticket for the bus was my ticket to a whole new world: the world of death and dying and of learning how best to stand with those who are awaiting their own bus.

STORIES NOT OF DEATH BUT OF LIFE

The stories related herein are stories of life rather than stories of death. These stories view life as a spiritual process that begins with birth, flows eventually to death, and continues on to a new life. Death is seen as a new kind of birthing.

This book addresses a variety of issues, such as grief and grieving, pain and suffering, letting go, the symbolic language of the dying, near-death experience, nearing death awareness, near-life experience, and learning how to listen to those who are on their way to death.

This book includes experiences of my own as a chaplain, a caregiver, and a bereaved husband. It also includes the stories of many people who are gone now, people who have, through their openness as they moved toward death, given us amazing glimpses of spiritual reality.

This book, as part of my present work with the dying, is driven by a firm belief in the value of story. It is from the stories of our lives that we find meaning and hope, or as master story-teller Father John Shea has said, we "tell, and retell" the stories "until we get them right." Shea's point is that the stories' details are secondary to the meaning that we attach to the stories. While the details may change, the meaning of the stories always remains the same, sharper each time we retell them, but the same.

Some of the stories I've collected here are my own. However, the bulk of this book comes from those who can no longer tell their own stories, those who have gone before us. And so, with a profound humility as we stand before the great "cloud of witnesses," I commit the audacious act of trying to speak for the silenced ones while protecting their anonymity by changing names and the details of certain circumstances.

LISTENING TO A DIFFERENT LANGUAGE

The language spoken by the dying may seem strange, new, and even frightening. Yet it is a language as ancient as Adam and

Eve, and as new as the person who died minutes ago, mumbling something about going home. To listen to the dying is to be informed that there is indeed a journey, that a destination looms ahead, and that death is not the end.

Listening well to people as they make the transition from this world to the next requires the ability to hear with and from the heart. We who are standing vigil must not prejudge what the dying person is saying. Instead we must attempt to listen with the purity implied in one dictionary's definition of hearing and listening: "To hear is to listen to and consider, to regard with favor, to give primacy to the person speaking, to value that which is being uttered; to listen is to heed what is being communicated, and to attend to its meaning."

To do anything less is to neglect not only what is being communicated but perhaps even the person conveying the message as well. This is precisely what occurs when a dying person speaks to us of visions and experiences and we, in turn, attempt to keep that person grounded in "reality."

As Elisabeth Kübler-Ross has observed, "If people would listen more to their own intuitive spiritual quadrant . . . they would begin to comprehend the beautiful symbolic language that dying patients use when they try to convey to us their needs, their knowledge and their awareness."[1] Creating that kind of a climate—a climate in which the dying are free to share the richness of their visions and those at the bedside are free to listen and open to hearing—is what this book is about. Perhaps in some small way this book may help us all to listen more carefully to the "intuitive spiritual quadrant" that exists within all of us and that the dying reveal through their words and faces.

A LOOK BEYOND THE OBVIOUS

A piece of fabric in a frame on the wall—that's all. Noticeable, but certainly not attention grabbing like a panoramic of Mount Rainier. I was told that if I stood a few feet away and relaxed, I would see a picture *within* the fabric. "Reflection is the key," said my brother-in-law and owner of the computer-designed geometric print known as Magic Eye art.

Not wanting to be antisocial, I played along. The longer I stood there seeing nothing but the fabric in the frame on the wall, the dumber and more challenged I felt. I never doubted that he could see what I could not. Yet I was becoming convinced that whatever he and others were seeing was a vision quite open to interpretation.

Then it happened. My daughter Kelly stood beside me. I glanced at her reflection, blinked my eyes, and saw a three-dimensional underwater scene: a huge wide-mouthed shark and smaller fish, a skull, a treasure chest, and an ocean-bottom garden. This picture that was a half inch deep had become a view of an ocean floor that was at least twenty-seven cubic feet in dimension.

The miracle is that once you've seen it, you cannot un-see it. You can lose the vision for a moment, but you can always go back to it and see it again. With new eyes, in a sense, you can hold on to the vision for as long as you want.

If I have learned anything from the dying, it is that we learn nothing by focusing on the obvious, such as what seem to be hallucinations. If we remain fixed on the presumed reality that the dying are out of their head's due to the morphine, and if we don't even attempt to communicate with them about their experiences, their visions, and their present realities, then we miss out on crucial information. If we do not step back and assist dying people in their own reflections upon what has become so obvious to them, all of us lose.

Caregivers—whether family or professional, in the home or in a care center—are often so deeply enmeshed in the intensity of care (trying to feed a person who really wants no food, turning a patient to avoid bedsores, helping a patient who just wants to be left alone, or administering medications routinely to a patient who routinely refuses them) that they do not see or hear what the dying are trying to convey to them.

Often, we caregivers are so overwhelmed with the obvious issues of health and comfort that we don't pick up the subtleties of language, whether verbal or nonverbal. There may simply be no time for it; it goes right over our heads. However, it does help to know that the dying often speak in metaphorical language, a most symbolic language, and we need to know that something is going on here. The meaning may not be obvious, but it is certainly present. As caregivers we need to at least note what is happening. Even if we are unable to pursue it further with the dying person, it will surely contribute something of immeasurable value to our own grieving process.

THE SPIRITUAL CONNECTION

The carefully constructed Magic Eye art can be experienced as a theological statement. As I stood there, eyes fixed on the obvious (the fabric in the frame on the wall), I began to appreciate why the disciples were so amazed that Jesus was walking on the water (Mark 6:45–52) and why Mark said that they simply did not understand the miracle of the loaves and fishes (Mark 6:34–44). "On the contrary, their hearts were hardened" (Mark 6:52). Even having observed Jesus perform the miraculous feeding, they really did not expect to see anything like it again.

The disciples, like all of us, were conditioned to seeing reality one way. They were accustomed to seeing Jesus as the son of Joe and Mary rather than as the Son of God. Social conditioning, then and now, leads us to see reality one-dimensionally: good and bad, black and white, secular and sacred, male and female. But Jesus was a person of many dimensions. His own mother was said to have pondered the events of his life in order to understand what all of it meant. The disciples, too, learned eventually to reflect on, and learn from, the events in the life of their teacher.

Reflection is the key to seeing beyond the obvious, to seeing the three-dimensional within the one-dimensional, and to seeing the new dimensions within the very fabric of our own lives. As we stand before the sacred stories on each ordinary day, we can either see the one-dimensional words or we can look beyond the obvious and experience spirituality that offers us more dimensions and more understanding.

To listen to the dying is to learn this sort of reflection. The dying person is speaking from the very depths of heart and soul. He or she is trying to convey what is being seen, heard, and felt. We, in turn, must hear with the heart. We must recognize that we are truly on holy ground; we are residing in a moment that is pregnant with divine drama.

CHAPTER TWO

listening and letting go

•

*i*n the movie *Shadowlands,*[1] C. S.
Lewis (Anthony Hopkins) comments to his wife, Joy, that our
experiences in this life are but shadows of those that await us in the
life to come. As the dying process kicks into gear, the dying person
often begins to see these shadows ever so clearly. It seems that, for
some people, shadows of individuals and places become oddly present. As the dying process begins to accelerate, these shadows
become more and more real: real people (usually deceased) and real
places. In the final stage, the shadows have become people and
places that are visible only to the person who is approaching the
end of life.

Often the shadowland experiences play a profound role in enabling the dying person and his or her loved ones to accept the fact of approaching death. These final moments can become family treasures, stories to be repeated by generations to come.

Occasionally the shadowland is so terribly frightening to the dying, and consequently disturbing to their loved ones, that our experience with it becomes more like a family secret to be locked away in the attic of memory. Yet, by listening well to the dying one's words and paying attention to nonverbal cues, we may find that even the most unsettling final moment of life can become a rich treasure to be taken from memory's attic and placed proudly on the family mantle.

"IT'S TIME TO GO"

While I am making rounds in the intensive care unit, my beeper goes off. I dial the number that comes up on the screen. The charge nurse in oncology informs me that a patient has requested a chaplain. The patient's family is gathered in her room. She wants a chaplain to pray with them.

As I enter the room, I am struck by how many people are sitting, standing, or leaning against the walls. A very large woman sits upright in the hospital bed. She is very much in charge here. With jet-black hair and dressed in a bright red housecoat, she looks as if she just stepped out of the beauty parlor. Her hair is unusually dark for a woman in her late fifties, and I soon realize that this is an oncology patient and the hair must be her wig.

She tells me to call her Marian and introduces each of the family members present. Then she cuts to the chase: "I'm dying.

I know that. I would appreciate it a great deal if you would lead us all in prayer while everyone is here and while I can enjoy it."

The room goes incredibly silent. Time seems to stop. The only sounds are the low whirring of the heating unit over by the window, Marian's somewhat labored breathing, and a sniffle here and there around the room.

As I stand here, I marvel at this apparent matriarch who has most likely orchestrated her family's life from A to Z. Now she is orchestrating her own requiem. Here is a woman who has exercised great power over the life of her family. She is now invoking perhaps even greater power out of her own brokenness. Taking a deep breath, I walk over to her bedside, take her hand, and state the obvious: "You seem very much at peace with your dying, Marian."

"I've had a good life, a wonderful life, a wonderful family. We can't live forever. We all have our appointed time. It is now my time. Yes, I am ready. I feel at peace with my family and my God. It's time. And now, it's time to pray."

I have never met a queen, but I feel as if I am in the presence of one now—a "priest" in her court, at least for the moment. Queen Marian has given the unmistakable cue: "It's time to pray!" Immediately after the prayer Marian says to no one in particular, "There! Now I'm ready to go."

One of the daughters asks, "Go where? You mean home? Remember, Mom, it's no longer possible for you to go home. But when the doctor says it's okay, you'll come to our home."

Marian, smiling broadly with a twinkle in her eye, looks directly at her daughter and responds, "No, I mean I'm ready to go with Dad. He's getting impatient, you know."

I hear a gasp here, a sniffle there. Another daughter exclaims, "Mom, Dad died. Remember?"

Marian, still smiling, says, "I know, but he's been around a lot lately, and I think it's about time I went with him. He's been pacing around this room and tapping his fingers on the edge of this bed. It's time to go."

A tissue box is being passed around the room for about the third time since we began the prayer. A son goes over to his mother, sits on the edge of her bed, and holds her close without saying a word. Another son explains to me, "Dad always was a pacer and would often tap his fingers on a table or the arm of a chair."

No one questions Marian any further. Instead they talk about Dad and his impatience. They talk about Mom and Dad and how they always did everything together. They talk about the memories. They reflect on what it all means.

As I remember that scene, it appears that Marian's body was telling her a great deal. She knew at a conscious level that death was on its way. At some subconscious level, perhaps, Marian knew that death was quite imminent. She was ready, and she wanted her family to prepare well for her departure. The family had been focused on the obvious: a mother who continued to be in charge; a mother who looked, sounded, and acted as she always had; and a doctor's word that she would soon be released. Here was a mother who was being a mother up to the very end: preparing her children, inviting them to look beyond the obvious and enter into a necessary stage of the grieving process. Unfortunately, the family only had a few hours to experience their anticipatory grief.

Marian died, alone, early the next morning. We can only surmise that Dad stopped his pacing, took Marian by the hand, and the two of them walked as a couple into the Shadowlands.

"I SEEN YOUR DADDY, SONNY"

In the movie *A Family Thing*,[2] starring Robert Duvall and James Earl Jones, there is a delightfully poignant scene depicting the mystery of symbolic language. As the film opens, Duvall's character, Earl, is at his place of business, a rental shop in a small southern town. Earl's nephew, Sonny, and Earl's father are helping at the store.

The phone rings, and Sonny answers. From the brief glimpse we have of Sonny on the phone, we get the impression that something is not right. "It's Aunt Ruby. Granny's fixin'. . ." He hesitates, looking down at the floor. "It's almost time."

The scene shifts to a modest home as Earl's pickup pulls into the driveway. Ruby, Earl's wife, is standing on the front porch leaning against a white column, waiting for Earl, Sonny, and her father-in-law to come within earshot. "She's been talkin' out of her head, Earl. She's been askin' fer ya."

We are now transported into a bedroom. In the bed lies a wizened woman shaking with the tremors of Parkinson's disease. Her head moves from side to side as she talks. Her arms and hands move about sometimes willfully, but mostly involuntarily without apparent purpose or direction.

Granny, with a radiant smile, says, "I seen your Daddy, Sonny. He's here."

"Granny, he's dead," Sonny responds with a look of bewilderment.

"No he's not. He's out back building me a shed to put my stuff in," she says with certainty.

While Earl and his mother are alone, she talks to him about looking after the family when she is gone. Earl responds with a denial of the obvious: "You're going to live to be a hundred, Momma. You're going to live a lot of years yet." Facing her son's halfhearted denial head-on, she retorts, "I'm eighty-five years old. That's plenty of stayin' alive to do."

Again, with a broad smile stretched across her emaciated face, Granny shares "the strangest dream" with her son. As she relates the dream, we observe Earl close-up; he is sitting at her bedside with his head bowed. Granny, absorbed in telling her dream, no longer looks at her son but gazes toward the ceiling.

"There I was down by the river, hanging my laundry on a branch of a tree. Ain't that the silliest thing?"

Earl smiles, gazing at the floor. Then he appears to realize what we have already observed: that Granny's involuntary and continuous movements have ceased. Granny is dead.

Earl rises from his chair, leans over his mother's body, whispers something we do not hear into her ear, and leaves the room. Entering the kitchen, where the rest of the family is waiting, Earl struggles with his emotions, choking back his tears, and finally blurts out, "Granny's gone, gone to heaven."

The room goes silent. Earl's daughter, who moments before was totally absorbed in her own world, now stands stunned with disbelief.

Earl's dad is sitting this whole time with his back to Earl. The announcement of his wife's death does not appear to impress him. "When's that coffee goin' to be ready?" he says. Earl regards his dad with apparent bewilderment and walks out onto the porch.

In this fictitious situation, there are many family issues to be resolved. While the movie does not depict Granny's shadowland experience as part of the family treasure, we can only surmise that her final dream would be told and retold for generations to come. We find out later that Granny has revealed a secret to the family pastor, thus setting the stage for Earl and others to deal with the family's dirty laundry. In retrospect, it becomes fitting that her final vision was of her hanging out laundry, down by the river.

"MICK, KEEP HAMMERING ON THE WALL!"

On my way home at the end of the day, I stop for a brief visit with a new hospice patient. The door opens, and I am greeted by a very pleasant woman in her middle forties, of moderate height but powerfully built with broad shoulders. Angela ushers me in with a warm welcome.

The room is dark. All the shades and drapes are closed. Angela invites me to take a seat at the dining-room table, where her husband is seated. Jim is tall, lanky, and muscular, with a perpetual smile.

In a few minutes, the conversation turns to Harley, our patient. Angela notes that Harley has been restless all day and just got to sleep a half hour ago. Assuring her that I will not disturb him, that I will return another time, I ask if we could just talk for a few minutes. "What can you tell me about Harley?" I ask.

Jim and Angela both begin talking. Jim backs off, and Angela continues with the revelation that her brother "has not had it easy." An itinerant carpenter, Harley provided well for his family but paid dearly with the decline of his own health and hearth. Being away from home and family seemed to take its toll on his marriage and on his relationship with his children. His wife is seeking a divorce. The cancer and the treatments have been devastatingly difficult for him physically, but the divorce seems to be destroying the very spirit and heart of this proud man. "We don't know why he hasn't died before now," Jim says.

"Is there anyone in the family who might be hanging on to him?" I ask. Immediately I am astonished at what I have just heard myself say! I do not, as a rule, ask this kind of question this early in the process of situational assessment. Usually I gather more information about the family or patient and establish more trust between the others and myself before I introduce this issue. It is as if someone else had asked the question, someone unseen by the three of us here. But, having gone this far, I decide to take it another step: "Someone who may find it very difficult to let him go?"

There is a long moment of silence. At first, I wonder if they heard my question. Do they understand what I am asking? Is the concept too foreign to their ears? Are these two most gracious and polite people trying to figure out how to say, "What the hell are you talking about?"

Finally, after what feels like an eternity, Angela responds somewhat hesitantly: "I'm not sure. . . ." She appears to be searching the darkened living room for an answer to my question. Her eyes float from one spot to another before fixing on a position just beyond my left shoulder. It's all I can do not to turn around to see what she's looking at.

"Well," says Jim. "I think we all know Harley is dying. There is nothing any of us can do to stop that. He knows he is dying. I think he is ready to go. He has been in so much pain. I don't know of anyone who would want to keep him around at this point."

As Jim is speaking, I notice that his eyes have fixed on the same spot Angela had chosen to look for answers. I am very aware that married couples often acquire each other's phraseology, habits, manners of speaking, and nonverbal styles of communicating—but picking the same spot in the room to stare at? This is really interesting!

Once again I feel compelled to turn toward the focus of this couple's stares. I decide to make an inconspicuous move and shift my chair slightly away from the table and in the direction of the spot to my left. Suddenly a deep voice emerges from the dark: "Me. I do!"

Turning now—jumping really—I can barely make out the form of a human being standing behind me in the dark corner on the other side of a room divider.

"This is Mick, Harley's son," says Jim. "This whole thing is very difficult for you, isn't it, Mick?"

A young man about six feet tall and probably about 250 pounds emerges slowly from the darkness and sits down with us at the table. He is wearing black pants, a black and yellow Pittsburgh Steelers jacket, a black Pittsburgh Pirates baseball cap, and black sunglasses. No wonder I haven't seen him in this dark room!

"You said, 'I do,' Mick. How do you mean that?" I ask.

Mick is slouched in his chair, holding his head in his right hand. At first he remains silent. Angela intervenes: "Mick, did you hear the chaplain's question?"

She turns to me and says, "Mick had a serious accident a few years ago. His hearing, among other things, was seriously affected."

"I heard, Aunt Angie. I mean, if Dad dies, I die!"

Mick's right hand becomes a symbolic revolver; he raises his index finger to his temple, cocks his thumb straight up in the air, and suddenly brings it down. His head droops to his chest.

This routine visit has now turned into something quite different. This young man is expressing suicidal ideation, and I have the moral and legal obligation to assess the seriousness of Mick's pain. For the next two hours I listen to issues of fear and anger, attempting to discern his readiness to commit the final act.

Mick recounts how important his father has been to him, especially after the auto accident, in which Mick was hurled through the windshield. Jim and Angela affirm that he came very close to death and explain how the doctors predicted that, should he survive, he would spend the rest of his days in a state of paralysis. He did survive. His father had been there at his bedside for days on end. His dad had pulled him through.

But survival had come at a cost. Mick would never regain his sharp mind. The head injury sliced into his ability to solve problems in the efficient manner for which he had become known and valued by his friends and relatives. Mick, once the fluent articulator, now speaks with halting, sometimes painful, deliberatation and does not always choose the appropriate words. Before the accident, Mick was a skilled carpenter, apprenticed under his father and looking forward to someday running his own construction company.

"But now," says Mick, "all I'm good for is mowing other peoples' lawns, and that takes me twice as long as a twelve-year-old girl! My dad has kept me going. After he dies there is no point to my not going with him. Let the twelve-year-old girls do it. I'm no good to anybody. Even my wife and daughter have left me. I'm no good to anybody, nobody."

Mick is sobbing, his body shaking as if he has just come in out of the winter cold. He removes his baseball cap and holds it to his face, soaking up the tears. In his Steelers/Pirates garb, he reminds me of the photo of a pitcher sitting on the bench, having just thrown the pitch that lost the World Series for his team. Angela tries to comfort him by noting how his lawn-mowing customers applaud his care and thoroughness as well as his dependability and adds, "besides, Amy probably would have left you anyway."

Mick responds as if on cue: "Auntie, most of my customers just feel sorry for me. And I don't care if Amy was going to leave me. I still love her, and I miss her and my little girl. Auntie, when Dad dies, I lose it all." The longer he talks, the angrier he becomes. His voice becomes sharp and high-pitched. He takes off his sunglasses and slams them on the table. "It just ain't fair!"

Thinking that Mick is perhaps angry with God for doing all this to him and to his father, I ask, "What is it that is the most unfair, Mick?"

Without hesitating, this young man, facing one of the darkest days in his life, reveals his real pain: "It's not fair that Dad is going to die without apologizing to me first."

"Apologize for what?"

"For telling everyone I'm just a vegetable." Mick stutters over the word. "And that I will never be any good to anybody!"

"You have heard your dad say those things to others?"

"Yes, I have. And so have Aunt Angie and Uncle Jim."

"Mick, you indicated that you might shoot yourself. Is that what you have in mind? Do you have a gun?"

"Well, I don't have a gun here. But I'm going back home to Oklahoma to get it, so when Dad dies I'll be ready." Mick says this to me as if he were going back to Oklahoma to pick up his best suit. He does have a plan. While he does not have the immediate means of carrying out the plan, he seems intent on doing so when the time is right.

For about thirty minutes I try to get Mick to agree that he will not take his own life. He stubbornly holds out, hanging on, perhaps, to this one last thing over which he has some control. Finally, he agrees only that he will not attempt his own life until after Harley dies.

Before leaving the premises, I walk into the bedroom and attempt to waken Harley. He rouses slightly. I introduce myself to him, and recognizing a very weak man when I see one, a person who may lose consciousness at any moment, I launch into Mick's dilemma. "Harley, your son is saying that when you die he is going to commit suicide. Can you find the energy to talk to him about that? If you want, I can help with the communication."

Harley appears to have slipped off again. I stand here looking at a person who can at best maintain a few moments' connection with the world. Here is a man whose own physical suffering is at an apex, even with hospice intervention working to control the physical pain. Will my intervention bring unwelcome tidings and aggravate the agony? I am not at all sure that my comment even registered. I stand here at this bedside wondering what I have done and what I should do.

To my surprise, Harley grabs my hand and says very weakly, "I can't. I can't do it anymore." His grip loosens, and he returns to a deep sleep.

I leave this troubled home with a less-than-perfect contract for life in my hand. Jim walks me out to the car. I tell him what Harley has just told me about not being able to do it anymore. Now Jim tells me that Mick has attempted suicide in the past. Twice Harley has rescued his troubled son from a lake in Oklahoma. Twice a young man who could not swim attempted to drown himself; and now a dying father no longer has the energy to jump into the troubled waters of his son's life.

Late that evening, the telephone rings; it is our on-call nurse. "Harley has been rushed to the hospital with a severe hemorrhage," she says. "His sister has requested your presence."

By the time I arrive at Harley's intensive care room, he has stabilized and is no longer considered at risk of dying—at least not tonight. Mick seems calm, and that scares me. Has he already made up his mind? Is he scheming some other means to end his life? He claims that he is okay and that he will do nothing tonight, except stay at his father's bedside. Angela will stand the vigil as well. Mick agrees to have breakfast with me tomorrow morning at the hospital cafeteria.

Early the next morning, after a sleepless night, I return to Harley's bedside. Mick and I are talking when, to our surprise, Harley comes out of his semicoma. At first he murmurs but then says, clear as day, "Mick, go get my hammer, some nails, and boards."

Mick lowers his voice and asks me, "What should I say?"

"Go with the flow, Mick. Just tell him you will get his hammer, some nails, and boards."

"OK, Dad. I'll do that. Anything you say, Dad."

I take Mick by the arm and walk him out of the room. "Let's have some coffee or something down in the cafeteria."

Neither of us is hungry. We have our coffee and talk. Mick seems to be in a better place: teary and downcast, but more relaxed. He even talks about plans after his father's death of expanding his lawn-mowing business to include snow removal.

"Do I hear you saying that life might be worth living after all?" I ask. "Are you able to let your dad go on to his Lord without hearing the apology from his lips?"

"Yeah, I guess," Mick says. His strength of conviction leaves much to be desired. However, he is planning a life for himself after the death of his father.

As we ride the elevator from the cafeteria to the intensive care unit floor, Mick asks, "What should I say to Dad now?"

"Well, respond honestly to anything he says. But make sure you tell him that the hammer, nails, and boards are ready. See where it goes from there. You might ask him what you should do with it all."

Mick speaks to his father: "Dad, how ya doing?"

Harley opens his eyes.

"We've got the hammer, nails, and boards, Dad. What now?"

"Mick, keep hammering on the wall." Harley's voice becomes weaker with each word. "Keep hammering on the wall. Mick, keep hammering on the wall. Mick, keep hammering . . . Mick, keep . . . Mick . . ."

With this mantra on his lips, Harley dies.

Harley could not find the energy to enter into an extensive and painful discussion with his troubled son. It was beyond his power to plead with Mick once again to not commit suicide. Harley did, however, tap into the power of metaphor to communicate with his son on a deep and personal level. He knew subconsciously that this was his last chance to save his son's life.

Mick never heard his father say in words, "I love you" or "Forgive me," but he continues to hammer at the wall of life and love, knowing that his father's love did not give up on him and never will.

"KEEP THEM AWAY!"

It's a beautiful spring day, sunny and cloudless. Driving up the gently winding street that follows the contour of the bluff, I notice the forsythia exploding with their rich yellow leaves, as if every other yard on this incline has its own sun.

However, most of the houses where I am headed are crowded together. The yards are small to nonexistent and so muddy that even dandelions are absent. The homes up here are replicas of each other: two-story frame houses with small porches straddling the front door, one window on each side. In a neighborhood without garages, cars haphazardly line the street.

A young woman in her early twenties greets me from the door as I step up to the porch. This is Carrie, Margaret's daughter. Carrie says she saw me drive by and noticed the hospice sticker on my rear window. "Are you always this prompt? You said you would be here at 10:30, and it was 10:30 when I saw you drive by."

"Well, I try. I would have made it, but finding a parking space around here is a bit of a challenge today."

"That has always been a problem here. Mom wants to move to a place where she can park her car in her own driveway. She has been talking about that for years. Maybe when she gets her medical bills paid she can start looking again."

When she gets her medical bills paid, she can start looking again? I have not yet met Margaret, our new hospice patient. I know very little about her, but I do know this: she is a forty-two-year-old woman with end-stage cancer of the colon, and the cancer has metastasized to her liver. From the reports I have heard from our nurse and social worker, this patient will be a short term on hospice—less than a week at best. Margaret may be getting herself a different place, but it will not be in Council Bluffs.

Carrie takes me inside and introduces me to her two-year-old daughter, Stacey, her friend Valerie, and her grandmother Wanda (Margaret's mother, I presume). Lying on the couch in this dark and crowded room is the skeletal form of a human being. Margaret is asleep, breathing irregularly and with a pallor that verges on pale green. *This person is not going to be with us long,* I think, just as she awakens.

I introduce myself to Margaret as Carrie, Valerie, and Stacey leave the room. With Wanda's assistance, Margaret strains to raise herself into an upright position. I never really know how to start these conversations.

"What's happening, Margaret?"

"Oh, I'm just trying to beat this thing."

"So, how goes the battle?" I hope she doesn't see how surprised I am to hear her talking as if this thing can be beaten. Why am I surprised? After all, Carrie gave me a clue of what to expect: "When she gets her medical bills paid, she can start looking again!" Has she looked in the mirror lately? Has she compared her present self with the beautifully vibrant human being in the photograph sitting on the television? Denial is apparent, but there is more than denial here.

"Well, you know, they told me last week there is nothing more to be done, but I'm going to show them. I'm going to beat it."

I turn to Wanda and say, "Sounds like we have a fighter here."

She replies in a less-than-convincing manner, her eyes betraying the heartfelt pain of a mother: "She sure is. And if Margaret says she is going to beat it, beat it she will."

"Well, if you are Margaret's mother, you should certainly know."

"Oh, I'm not Margaret's mother! I am her divorced husband's mother. I always figured my son was stupid to lose Margaret. But that didn't mean I had to lose her. We have continued our friendship ever since the divorce ten years ago."

Twisting herself around, trying to find a more comfortable position, Margaret interjects, "Wanda has been like a mother to me; in fact, better than my own mother. My kids, Wanda, my coworkers are all important to me. They keep me going, and I'm going to beat it," she concludes. "Three more years; that's all I ask."

Now we are getting to it! Margaret is not so much denying her demise as she is bargaining with it. Something important to her will occur in the next three years; something important enough for her to willfully continue the long and painful fight. Can we talk about it, I wonder, especially with Wanda present?

"Margaret, I will certainly join in supporting you in your fight. And I will pray that you find the strength to do what you have to do, that your goal of at least another three years is realized. Sounds like a very important goal for you."

Margaret turns her head to the side, but her tears have already betrayed a distractive turn. "Very important," she says.

"You see, Toddy, my youngest—well, life has not been easy for her. Lots of trouble. You name it. Counseling, suspensions, arrests, depression, disastrous relationships. But now she is pulling herself out of it. She is in an alternative school. She will graduate from high school in December and wants to go to the community college. I told her I will be there when she gets that associate degree three years from now. I promised her. I promised myself. I pray every day that I can fulfill that promise."

As I sit here in the silence of a moment filled with poignant drama, I am torn. On the one hand, there is the desire that some miracle will enable this young mother to realize her goal; on the other, there is the felt need to yank her back from the menacing precipice of unrealistic hopes and expectations. All I can do is listen and try to help this agonized mother sort through her issues and feelings. In the end I may be able to do nothing that will help Margaret find her way through the bargain basement into which she has wandered.

Finally Margaret breaks the silence and says, "Besides, I'm afraid of dying. I'm not ready to die. I'm too young to die!" Simple statements filled with most complicated meaning.

"Being afraid and fearful about death and dying is quite normal, Margaret. Is there more you would like to say about your fears?"

"I'm afraid for my kids. No question. They're very dependent on me. I don't know what will happen to them. But . . ." Tears well up in her eyes, and her jaw begins to quiver. "I am too young to die. I'm not going to die, not yet. I'm going to beat this thing. I have a deal with God. I will beat it. I am just too young to die!"

"Kind of seems unfair, doesn't it, Margaret?"

"So damned unfair! But I am not going to die. I'm simply too young to die."

At this point I hear someone coming up to the front door, and suddenly the living room is full of people: Margaret's kids and their friends, their kids and their friends' kids. The place has become a public square. Communication with Margaret is about to become impossible. Can I salvage any last-minute quality exchange?

"Margaret," I ask, "would you like a short prayer before I go?" She nods, and I begin immediately, hoping to strike before this scene becomes bedlam itself.

"Dear God, I pray for Margaret and her family. We have a woman here who is a fighter. A woman who has so much to live for. We know that you indeed work miracles and wonders; the problem is sometimes we do not recognize your healing power at work. May Margaret, her family, and all those who love her, be attentive to your action in their lives. May Margaret find the strength in herself, in you, dear Lord, and in those who stand by her side to make this difficult journey."

"Margaret," I ask, "What is one thing you would like to pray for right now?"

Without hesitation Margaret proclaims, "That my children can make it on their own."

"Then I say Amen to that. Amen and Alleluia."

Margaret thanks me for coming. In the midst of what must be at least twelve adults, three crying infants, and now a barking dog, I take leave, wishing I had more time, more space. "Margaret, would it be okay for me to stop by sometime tomorrow? Maybe we could continue our conversation then."

"That would be fine. I would like that. Around 9:30 might be good. There should be fewer people here. On the other hand, I may be gone. There are a few things I need to do at the office, so call before you come."

"It's a deal, Margaret." I pick my way through the crowd to the door, wondering as I go, *How can she think she can go to her office when she cannot, on her own, even get to the bathroom ten feet from her couch? This bargain she has with her God, whatever it is, is something we need to talk about tomorrow.*

For Margaret, however, there is no tomorrow. At 11:45 this evening, approximately twelve hours after I left Margaret's home, my phone rings. It is our on-call nurse. "Margaret has expired," Diane tells me, "and the family would like you to come. They don't understand what has happened here, and I'm not sure I do either. I'll be watching for you and will fill you in when you arrive."

Most people, when they get as close to death as Margaret obviously was twelve hours ago, are "hearing" their bodies tell them that the time is near. Apparently this was not the case for Margaret. As best I could tell, she really believed she would get better. And her family? Did they too believe what she believed? Is this the issue I am going to have to deal with, a family in total and absolute shock?

Walking up the block to Margaret's house, I notice someone sitting on the front porch. It is Diane. She gets up and comes down the street to greet me. "Ron, I've never seen anything like it! Of course, since we have had this patient for only a day, I really knew little about what I was getting into when I got the call from the caregiver. But this one really takes the cake. This one is spooky!"

"What do you mean?"

"Well, when I arrived, she was out of it, breathing very hard with fifteen-second periods of apnea, mottling up to the knees; and then all of a sudden . . ." Diane's voice trails off. She stops and seems to shudder. I take her by the arm and notice that, despite the warm evening, she has goose bumps.

Diane relates how this patient, who appeared to be well on her way in the active dying process and completely immobile, suddenly raised herself up on her right elbow. Pointing with her left arm and extending her index finger toward the door to a hallway, she screamed out with the entire family standing at her side, "NO!! NO!! Keep them away! I'm not ready to go!" With that, Margaret collapsed and died.

"I think that is what the family needs help with," Diane says. "It would have been easier for them if she had accepted that she was going to die, but obviously she could not."

There must be twenty people in the living room, sitting, standing, leaning, and holding one another. Wanda is here. She comes to greet me with tears cascading down her cheeks: "Has the nurse told you what happened here tonight?"

"Yes, she has. Was that frightening for you, for the family?"

"Very."

"This is our chaplain," Diane announces to the bewildered group.

"Diane has explained to me what happened just before your mother, grandmother, and friend died. I want to extend my deepest condolences to you all. If you would like to have a moment of prayer before the funeral director arrives, I would be pleased to assist with that. But I wonder if you might have any questions or concerns about what happened here tonight."

At first there is a long moment of silence, punctuated by sniffles and the blowing of noses. Finally, Wanda affirms that a family prayer is exactly what they had in mind when they asked Diane to call the chaplain.

From the hallway Margaret's son, Bill, asks, "What does it all mean? I mean, it was so strange; so bizarre; so, well, spooky. I thought Mom was already dead when she sat up and acted as if someone was here. She was scared. Our Mom was never scared of anything. But tonight she was scared. And damn it, so am I."

A number of other people are nodding. Some of them are weeping.

"Unfortunately, I met your mother for the first and last time this morning. You know her far better than I do. But the woman I met earlier today was deeply concerned about you all. After all, she was a mother, and that is her right, the right to worry about her family, the right to worry about those she loves. Margaret was not yet ready to go. She thought herself far too young to die, and I think we can all agree to that. What you witnessed tonight was very normal in the sense that many, if not most, people see someone come for them just moments before they die. I doubt your mother was afraid of those she saw; she was just not yet ready to go with them. I have no idea who it might have been that she saw. I am sure it was someone now deceased who had loved her a great deal when they were walking this Earth as you and I do. Any idea who that might have been?"

"Her parents," Wanda responds.

"Grampa," someone from behind me remarks.

"Yes," Wanda says, "my husband died three years ago. He really loved Margaret. In fact he never forgave my son for leaving Margaret and the kids. His last words before he died were, 'Tell Margaret I love her.'"

We all gather around Margaret's body and pray. At the end of the prayer, Bill interjects, "God, it's okay. We know Mom thought she had a deal with you, but we really knew that was her way of protecting us. It's okay. Just make sure you take good care of her now."

As I walk slowly back to my car, processing all that has gone on, I suddenly realize Margaret *did* know. Her body *was* telling her something. She *did* warn us. She *knew* she was not going to see this new day.

I recalled what Margaret said when I asked if I could return the next day: *On the other hand, I may be gone.* Everyone knew there was no way she could have gone to work. At some subconscious level Margaret had warned us. We had missed the reality by focusing on the obvious.

THE SPIRITUAL CONNECTION

"The Scriptures," notes Elisabeth Kübler-Ross, "are full of symbolic language."[3] She continues from there to urge her reader to pay close attention to the "beautiful symbolic language" of the dying. The stories related in this chapter illustrate the beauty of the language of the dying and its connection with Scripture.

Just as Jesus said within earshot of his disciples, "Father, the hour has come" (John 17:1), Marian said to her family, "It's time to go." Jesus' disciples, Marian's family, and Granny's and Margaret's families had no clue that the deaths of their beloved were so imminent. For Marian it was only a matter of hours before she would die; for Granny it was just a few minutes; for Margaret it was seconds; for Jesus it was but a few hours later that he was arrested in the Garden of Gethsemane and on his way to his death. Marian, Granny, and Jesus knew far more of their future than anyone around them did. All three knew that the hour had come, and they were ready for their departure.

Most of us will know when our hour has come, perhaps long before our loved ones, our physicians, or other professional caregivers are ready to accept it. Our bodies will communicate to us what those around us will continue to deny or ignore. Harley knew that his hour had come and that the only way he could communicate with his son was through the metaphor of building a wall. As Jesus promised in his last discourse, "I say to you, whoever believes in me will do the works that I do, and will do greater ones than these" (John 14:12). Perhaps Harley was promising Mick that he could do far greater work if he would just "keep hammering on the wall." Margaret, Harley, Granny, and Marian were all communicating symbolically what they could no longer express in overt and direct language to those gathered around them.

QUESTIONS FOR REFLECTION AND DISCUSSION

What do I need to do to prepare myself for the final hour? What part of myself do I see in Marian, Granny, Mick, and Margaret?

What is most difficult for me to let go of:
- my hopes and dreams?
- the things I value?
- the people I love?

⤳

CHAPTER THREE

hearing from the heart of near-death experience

*T*he literature on death and dying is full of stories, analyses, and speculations concerning episodes of near-death experience (NDE). In the works of Elisabeth Kübler-Ross, Melvin Morse, and Raymond A. Moody we encounter the miraculous experiences of thousands of people.[1] From these accounts we have been able to glean common characteristics of both the event of NDE and its apparent effect upon those who experienced it.

- Seeing a bright soft light
- Being drawn to the light and through a tunnel to a beautiful palace
- Hearing, and often seeing, deceased family and friends

- Hearing the voice of the Divine
- Receiving a direct command to return to life

Acquiring outstanding insights, becoming less materialistic, and becoming more contemplative are a few of the common characteristics that seem to define those who have gone beyond the brink and returned to tell the story. Perhaps the most common of all these characteristics, however, is a certain freedom from the fear of death.[2] Another trait of those who have experienced NDE is an understanding and acceptance of their own mortality. The reality is that even the person who has come close to death and survived will in fact die someday. So while a person who has seen death is no longer afraid of it, he or she has no illusion about being immortal.

Often, when we encounter people who know that they are terminal and who appear to be uniquely at peace with this concluding chapter of life, we have reason to suspect that they have "been there and done that." They have had a preview of things to come. They are not afraid of death but may be afraid to tell the story.

This chapter tells such stories.

"BEEN THERE AND DONE THAT!"

As I drove through the undulating hills and rich farmland toward a small town in southwest Iowa, I tried to imagine what Val would be like. I had heard from our nurse that this patient was "a character, one of a kind," a woman who had a special command of "colorful language." She had been a truck driver long before women were accepted in that profession and before the interstate highways were built. Mrs. Val Randolph, by definition, had to be tough. But I may have been lulled into defenselessness by the soft, almost lilting sound of her granddaughter's voice when I called to make the appointment.

"She would love to meet you any old time!" Lori had said in a distinctly southern drawl.

Now, as I enter their home, Lori moves immediately to my defense and explains, "Grandma, this is the hospice chaplain who called earlier. You agreed to see him, remember?" Lori intervenes with a skill that has, apparently, come with much practice. She is a refined person, about forty years old, attractively attired, with sparkling eyes and brunette hair done up in a French twist. She is sure in demeanor, sincere in approach, and seemingly secure in who she is in this world.

"I don't want anything, Mrs. Randolph," I respond, "other than just to meet you and get acquainted. As Lori said, I'm the hospice chaplain and I like to meet each of our—"

"No. No! No minister ever walked across the threshold of that door without wanting money. Now I want to know what *you* want."

Mrs. Randolph, tethered to an oxidizer, sits in the dinette. Her breathing is labored, even with the assistance of extra oxygen. She appears to be of the same lithesome build as her granddaughter, but with a considerably harsher approach to life.

Here is a person who has graduated from the school of hard knocks. She is a quick judge of character, and I am in her court.

"Well, I'm not a real minister," I hear myself saying. "I'm just a hospice chaplain."

She emits a boisterous laugh. "Well, you just take a seat right here, young man. How's about a beer?"

"You don't know how much I would really like a beer on a hot day like today, but I must not drink while I'm working."

A smile forms and broadens on her face. "Well, since you're not a real minister, I'm not offering you a real beer. How's about a Sharp's?"

"I'll take it!" The three of us have a good laugh.

"Well then, young man, what do you want to know about an old grouch like me?"

The picture is coming into focus now. Mrs. Randolph is, among other things, a person who enjoys putting strangers (or maybe just clergy) to the test. This is beginning to feel more like a game than a rigorous exam.

"I'm told that you've been an over-the-roader for many years. I would like to know how that was for you, especially how it is now to be cooped up in here after being free to travel far and wide for so long."

"Well, first of all, young fella, you're one of the few folks who ever use that term, other than us over-the-roaders, us truckers. But to answer your question: I hate this shit! Do you hear me? I hate it!"

Suddenly, she slams her fist on the table. The beer can jumps, and she grabs it out of the air like my great-aunt Lulu used to snatch flies. She is smiling an almost impish smile. I think she planned that little act just for my benefit.

"But this is the run I have to make now," she continues. "You know I drove in to and out of many terminals in my day. Now they tell me I'm it!" Taking another sip of beer, she looks over at me with a "go ahead and ask" look.

"They tell you you're it?"

"Yeah. That I'm terminal. But I got one more run to do. One more ride. One more weigh station to check in to before I get to the Big Terminal. That trip is coming up real soon. Yep, real soon." Taking another sip, she adds, "Real soon, but I'm in no damn hurry. I know the road will be bumpy, full of potholes, so I can wait for the Dispatcher to call me in!"

"Suppose the Great Dispatcher called you in tonight," I ask, somewhat hesitantly for effect.

"Well, hell, you don't got much choice. When the Dispatcher says go, you get your ass in the rig and go!"

"You mean you wouldn't even bargain for a delay?" I ask.

"Listen, sonny, I've talked myself out of a few runs in my day. But this time it's just plain different, real different. I'm not talkin' myself outa this one. No way. I don't have the energy to bargain, argue, or plead. In fact, it don't seem like such a bad deal. I know the route pretty well. Most days lately I just want to get on with it."

There is something about what she is saying that I find awfully intriguing. Actually, it is not what she is saying that is so beguiling; it is what she is not saying.

"Mrs. Randolph—"

"Just call me Val, will ya?"

"Val, I am hearing and seeing a person who is very much at peace with herself, her life, and with the trip ahead of her," I say, moving my chair slightly closer to her. "I mean, you seem content and ready to go whenever the Great Dispatcher says it's time to hit the road. I hope you don't take that for granted. Not everyone is as accepting of the final run as you are. How do you account for that?"

She doesn't hesitate at all, but looks me straight in the eyes and says, "Well, tell ya what. I should be okay with it all, 'cause I've been there and done that."

Val turns silent and reflective, and I decide to see where the silence leads us. I have become gradually aware of the sounds of silence: the oxidizer's low roar, the air conditioner's rattle and whir, Lori's cease-fire with the dirty dishes. Lori, I realize, has been listening in all this time. She, too, is eager to hear how her grandmother has "been there and done that."

"You see," Val continues, "some years ago, many years ago, I was on the operating table when things suddenly weren't going well. It was as if I were above the table. I was looking down at myself. I could hear the doctors and nurses talking about me. I knew it was not good. One doctor was frantic: 'We're losing her! We're losing her. God damn it! Get in here. Bring her back. Bring her back. Ah, shit!' And I could tell that one of the nurses was crying. Next thing I know I'm being drawn through this tunnel-like thing when everything goes black for a moment, followed by a light that gets brighter and brighter, a soft and warm light. Soon I see these beautiful palace-like buildings, and this wonderful, wonderful, inviting garden. Damn! It was soooo peaceful."

Val stops her retelling of this near-death experience. She is sitting quietly, and tears are rolling down her cheeks.

"Why did you come back?" I ask.

"Well, that's the part that really sucks! This voice told me to go back. 'You've got more work to do,' the voice said. I know it was God's voice. I didn't see him. Shit, I didn't see anybody, just the palaces and the garden. So, I came back." Val hangs her head and shakes it from side to side.

"Why do you say coming back sucks?"

"Because it is one thing to be told that I had more work to do, but the voice neglected to tell me what it was I had to do. And I still don't know! It has always pissed me off. I mean, do I have one more floor to clean before I've done what I have to do? What is it I have to do before I can go back and stay there permanently? I didn't get it then, and I don't get it now."

"Grandma, when did that happen?" Lori comes to the table and pulls up a chair at Val's side. "I never heard this story before. Wow!"

"Well, girl, not everyone thinks it is a 'wow'. When I told one of the nurses, she told me it was the anesthesia, just a hallucination. She laughed and walked away. The doctor, however, told me I did come very close to death. When I told him what I heard him say and how he looked, and that the nurse was crying, his eyes got real big. He turned a little pale and sat down on the edge of my bed."

Val sits quietly for a moment, as if trying to remember something. "When was it? Well, I don't recall month, date, and year. It was a long time ago. But I do remember one thing. It was while I was recuperating at home that your mother told me she was pregnant. I remember now. I had just gotten into bed after the trip from the hospital. She had never, not once, come to see me at the hospital, and I was in there for three weeks. Not once had she even stopped by the house to see how her father, your grandfather, was doing. But when I was exhausted to the core, she comes in and says, 'I'm gonna have a baby.' "

"Your near-death experience was somewhere around forty-two years ago, Grandma. I'm forty-one, and you took me in right after I was born."

"That's right. There was no way that daughter of mine could have raised you properly—not sure we did either, but you turned out mighty fine. Just wish you could have had a decent mother and father."

Turning to me now, Val looks puzzled. "I sure wish the Lord had been a little clearer about what I was supposed to come back to do. How is one to figure such things out?"

"I'm not sure, Val, but it sounds to me like the Lord probably knew your daughter was pregnant. God most likely knew, as you did, that Lori's mother could not do a proper job of nurturing. Is it not possible that the Lord sent you back to care for Lori?"

Lori begins to cry and embraces her grandmother. Val, nodding her head and sobbing, says, "I never thought of that. It was right in front of me all these years, and I never saw it."

One month later, Val went gently into the night. The Great Dispatcher called in her rig. She was ready and unafraid, having been there and done that before.

FLYING TO HEAVEN

The small private plane crashed in an Alaskan forest. Annie's husband and the pilot died instantly. The day after the crash a rescue team found her crumpled body lying in the midst of the wreckage. At first they thought she was dead. But she screamed in pain and terror when they moved her body. She was transported to a hospital in Anchorage, where it was then discovered that nearly every bone in her body was broken. If she survived it would be a miracle, and it would require massive medical intervention, extensive treatments, prolonged recuperation, and a Herculean will to live.

Annie and Jerry, a Mormon missionary couple, had been on their way to an Alaskan outpost to look over the general "lay of the land." Now Jerry was dead, as was their dream to serve their God and their church.

Miraculously enough, Annie's condition stabilized. Her parents asked that she be transferred closer to home and her two sons, who were living with their grandparents in Council Bluffs. Ultimately, Annie arrived at the medical center where I was chaplain.

Knowing something of the case, I was still blown away by what I saw when I first walked into Annie's room. The frailty of her body and the plethora of medical machines stunned me. *Yes,* I thought, *she has survived thus far, but how in God's name can she really survive? How can such a broken body have a fulfilling life? Will she ever be able to talk again?* The first night, and for many nights thereafter, I just sat at her bedside holding her unbroken hand, talking quietly to her, and praying while she remained motionless and silent. I wondered what it was like for her little boys to know that their father was dead and to see their mother so shattered.

Then, one night Annie murmured a "thank you" as I rose from my chair to leave. It was a weak but distinguishable response. Laying my hand upon her forehead, I said, "God bless you, Annie." She smiled and fell back to sleep.

One week later, Annie was talking freely, sitting up in bed, and feeding herself. There was no doubt now: Annie was going to make it. She had become our medical miracle. As I walked into her room, however, I saw that she was experiencing some nausea. Her mother and her sister were at her bedside. "If this is not a good time, I can return another time," I said.

"No, that's okay. I've been through worse than this," she said, holding the plastic container below her chin.

"Yes, you sure have. As a matter of fact, you have experienced something few people get to talk about."

Without looking up, she replied, "It was a beautiful experience."

Her mother gasped. "Beautiful? How can anything so horrible be beautiful?"

Ignoring her mother's understandable response and reaching over to take Annie's hand, I asked, "Is there more you would like to tell us about how it was beautiful for you?"

Without hesitation, Annie said, "I was flying with the animals, and it was so beautiful, so peaceful, so free." Her eyes sparkled. "So free. So free."

Stopping now and looking once again into the plastic receptacle on her lap, this survivor of a trip to hell seemed to be back in the Alaskan wilderness.

Long moments passed before I asked, "Where were you and the animals flying to, Annie?"

This young missionary, who now had to make calculated decisions to move any part of her body, immediately turned her head and sent a penetrating look into my eyes. Few times in my life have I felt someone other than myself search my soul. I shall never forget that intense gaze. It said very clearly, "Can I trust you?" Finally, she said, "We were flying to heaven." Annie smiled broadly then and looked at all of us. "And we almost made it."

I nodded in affirmation and reached to take her hand in mine. "Do you recall anything specific that you saw, heard, or felt? How far did you go?"

"Oh, so much. I think about it all the time. When I couldn't talk and everybody was doing everything for me, when I was so hurting and so discouraged, that is what kept me going. I kept going back to the beauty of the place in my mind. It was so peaceful there and so beautiful. There is no other word for it: The soft warm light that highlighted the rich landscape of flowers and flowering trees and bushes. So many animals resting, feeding, and frolicking. The gorgeous palace, huge, and so inviting. Monstrously big buildings usually scare me, but this one made me feel like I was home. I stood there at the door knocking and trying to open the door. I wanted so desperately to get inside where I knew I would be safe."

Her mother and sister were crying, but Annie recounted her near-death trip as if she were sharing an exciting vacation picture album. Indeed, we were, all three of us, getting the picture.

"It sounds so inviting," I said. "You have described what you saw so well, but I'm sure words just don't do it—kind of like trying to capture the Grand Canyon in one single shot with an old Brownie camera. But why did you come back?"

Annie glanced over toward her mother and then back to me. "Because Uncle Bob told me to. He said to me, 'Go back, Annie. Go back. You have more work to do. Go back, Annie.' He said it just like that. There are times when the pain and the loneliness are so great that I get really angry at myself for listening to him. But I do have more work to do. I need to raise my kids. And with God's help I will return to the missions."

THE SPIRITUAL CONNECTION

They that hope in the LORD *will renew their strength,*
  they will soar as with eagles' wings;
They will run and not grow weary,
  walk and not grow faint.

ISAIAH 40:31

Annie's NDE reassured her that death, whenever it does come to visit her, is not something to fear. Annie can now embrace death simply because she has been there and done that. Annie and Val obtained something else from their ordeals with imminent but unfulfilled death: reason and purpose to continue living. Annie had no problem identifying what she needed to do upon coming back from the brink of death and eternal life. Val spent years trying to make sense out of it all. Both Val and Annie received a common dividend from their individually unique near-death experiences: a removal of the fear of death. Their families have a common framework for understanding why and how Annie and Val survived to tell their stories and continue their journeys.

Val and Annie soared as with eagles' wings to a strange and beautifully enticing land, but they, like Lazarus (John 11) and Jairus's daughter (Mark 5:22–43; Luke 8:41–56), were told to return to the living, to their families. Each of them had more work to do. From that moment on they could say about death:

"Been there and done that!" When the reality of death and the finality of life do come to Val and Annie, they will be unafraid. They will be ready to "soar as with eagles' wings" to a new land briefly seen before.

QUESTIONS FOR REFLECTION AND DISCUSSION

How does Annie's experience influence our theology?

What is my vision of heaven?

What does it mean to "hear with the heart"?

CHAPTER FOUR

listening for

the silent witnesses

Since the 1992 publication of Callanan and Kelley's *Final Gifts*,[1] there has been a growing awareness of the correspondence between near-death experience (NDE) and the different types of awareness that the dying acquire as the reality of inescapable death approaches. The latter has become known as nearing death awareness (NDA). The difference between NDE and NDA is that often the person having an NDA is able to communicate something of the experience while it is happening. Unfortunately, people rarely share their NDA or NDE experiences for fear that they will not be taken seriously.

This chapter shall focus on an event of the dying that is so common it is nearly predictable: the profound experience of seeing deceased friends, relatives, or even a God figure at one's bedside. These episodes, while typically nonthreatening to the dying person, are almost always puzzling—and sometimes frightening—to those who are gathered at the bedside.

While our understanding of this part of the dying process has grown since the 1960s, the experience itself is perhaps as old as the human race. We have historical, anecdotal data indicating that the perceived presence of deceased loved ones at the deathbed is an ancient event that transcends all cultures.[2]

For Christians, the NDA makes all kinds of sense. It is the lived reality of the "cloud of witnesses" (Hebrews 12:1), or what we call the communion of saints. For Mormons, it is the presence of the saints. For Native Americans, it is the unity of life, the way things are connected in the circle of life. For those who understand what is happening, it is a most comforting and reassuring event. For those who do not understand the dying when they speak of a mysterious presence, it is disconcerting.

This chapter tells the story of several such episodes, as well as instances where those standing at the bedside did see at least the shadows of a presence.

"COME TO MOMMA!"

Dee's call is a frantic one. She is terribly frightened and admits that she's nearly paralyzed by the "strange goings-on" around her mother's bed. Something is happening with her mother that she does not understand. Her mother, Sheila, is saying some strange things and apparently seeing some strange people as well.

I can hear the hesitation and fear in Dee's voice and can almost see the bewilderment in her face, which is ninety miles away from me. "What is your mother saying, Dee?" There is a long pause at the other end of the line, but I can hear soft sobbing.

Finally, a tear-choked voice says, "Mom just keeps pleading, 'Come to Momma! Come to Momma! Come to Momma!' She repeats that over and over again, always as if there's a child off to the side of the room. But then, it's as if she's talking to someone at the foot of her bed, someone she calls 'Sis.' Chaplain, I have never been so scared in my life! Could you possibly come?" Dee's only other companion at the moment, a little ball of white fur known as Spike, is not helping much. I can hear Spike barking and whining in the background.

I assure Dee that I am on my way, but I know that it will take more than an hour to get out there on this wintry night. I attempt to reassure her that what is happening is very normal. We do not as yet understand exactly what it is that her mother is experiencing. But in her own way she is embracing what many dying people encounter. "Take a deep breath, Dee. Put on a pot of coffee. Have one on me, and I'll be there by eight. Just have a cup waiting for me. We will talk. It's okay to be frightened. But your Mom is okay. You're okay. You're doing a great job of caring for her, and you're doing the right thing by calling here."

As I drive through the darkness, I realize that Dee is at the moment doing the same. The difference, perhaps, is that I have headlights and she does not. According to what I know, Dee is isolated from her siblings. She is the only child from her mom and dad's marriage. Her siblings from her mom's first marriage have made it abundantly clear to our hospice staff that Dee's dad may be *her* father, but he is *not* part of the family; and she is certainly not *their* sister. I wonder aloud, "Does Dee have any support at all? Where does she get the strength to hang in there?"

Dee is a woman in her late twenties who appears to be about twice her age. Her jet-black hair is drawn back with a white bow and hanging down to her shoulders. Her brownish-toned and high-cheek-boned face is also drawn, and it looks as if something deep inside is tightening her very soul. Her life has not been easy or pretty. Yet Dee is now the primary caregiver for her dying mother. She is scared and mostly alone in the midst of a highly dysfunctional family.

Having made it to my destination, I notice that Dee is standing at the door with Spike in her arms. I am struck by the apparent urgency of Dee's very being. She is suddenly at my side when I emerge from the car, and she is crying. Spike is licking her face.

We walk inside, and two freshly poured cups of coffee are sitting on the table just inside the door. Dee motions for me to sit. "If you don't mind, I just want to talk before we go in to see Mom."

"That's pretty much what I had in mind. Your mother probably knows what is going on, but I gather you do not, and that is really frightening to you. But tell me, have you been able to make any more sense out of what your mother seems to be experiencing?"

Dee looks at me over the top of her coffee cup and with a visible shudder replies, "No. No, I haven't. And, frankly, I'm scared to walk down that hallway."

At this moment Spike jumps from Dee's lap and runs down the hallway leading to Sheila's bedroom. Within seconds, Spike is barking and yipping as if frightened by what he sees. I wonder if the little mutt has picked up Dee's fear—or if he is seeing what Dee cannot see.

"It's like *that,* dear God!" Dee exclaims. "I swear, Spike sees something or someone in that room other than my mother. And I don't see anything or anybody, but I feel it. You may think I'm nuts, but whatever Mom is seeing . . ." Dee's voice breaks, and she clutches the coffee cup with both hands, "is real. Mom is not alone in that room, and I think Spike knows that. I think Spike and Mom are seeing the same thing."

"I can understand why you're so afraid. But tell me, did your mother ever lose a child to death, either at birth or shortly thereafter?"

"No. All she ever had was me by my dad, and my three stepsisters and my stepbrother by her first husband. That's all she ever had, just the five of us. I know what you're thinking, so I'll tell you right now: No, my mother had no sisters. In fact, she was an only child. So I just don't have a clue who this 'Sis' is—this person she's talking about—I mean talking to, or whatever."

"It may seem strange, but many people, as they are approaching the end, see people who have loved them a lot, people who are deceased. I think that is happening here with your mother. Who she is seeing is simply not clear to us. Have you asked her who it is she is talking to?"

"No, I haven't. But she isn't responding much to me anymore when I do talk to her."

At this moment we hear Sheila's weak voice drifting down the hallway. Spike runs to the doorway, whimpers, and backs away, looking scared and confused. As we walk down the hallway, Dee picks up Spike and cradles him in her arms. I'm not sure who is comforting whom.

"Come to Momma, please come to Momma," Sheila repeats again and again.

Dee asks, "Who is it, Mom?"

No response. Sheila is sleeping.

As we leave the bedroom, the front door opens. Dee's father, Reggie, is arriving home from work. He pours the three of us a cup of coffee. Dee informs Reggie why I'm here, explaining that she was frightened by Sheila's talking to "Sis" and her repeated requests for someone to "come to Momma."

Reggie turns suddenly pale around the eyes as a look of shock registers on his face. The coffee cup shakes as he sets it down.

For a long moment, Reggie sits at the table and fingers the cup, looking blankly into the coffee as if he were trying to read tea leaves. Finally, he says, "Dee, I guess the time has come to tell you. Your mother did have another little girl about a year and a half before she married her first husband. Your mom would have been about sixteen at that time. The baby died about a week after birth. Your mom talked to me about it only once. She never wanted to discuss it again. It was too painful for her. She blamed herself for the death. She made it clear to me that I was never to bring it up again, nor were you or her other children to know about it. So I have tried to respect her wishes. But now, well I guess she has opened it up."

Reggie drinks from the cup and continues. "As for 'Sis,' well, the fact is your mother did have a sister. Elena apparently was a wild one. Got into drugs and lots of trouble. Your mother's family disowned her. As far as I know they destroyed every picture of her. She took off to California years ago. No one has ever heard from or about her. She has been presumed dead for some time. But no one in your mother's family has ever talked about her since I have known them. Well, once they did in my presence, but they never used her name."

"What you're telling me, Dad, is that when Mom says 'Come to Momma' she is probably seeing that little girl of hers! And 'Sis' is Elena!"

Two days later Sheila's last words were, "We can go now." And go she did, we presume, hand in hand with Elena and the little girl who finally had come to Momma.

Sheila's experience is, in a sense, run-of-the-mill. The phenomenon is so widespread that volumes could be written detailing the individual and always unique events that surround it. These are back-to-the-future episodes if there ever could be such an authentic irony. Sheila's little girl and her deceased sister were clearly sightings from the past. The consequence of those sightings for Sheila was a lightening of the load, a lessening of worry and fear, a straightening of the road as she prepared for the biggest journey of all, knowing that she would not be alone in making the trek to the beyond.

Marian (chapter two) did not say directly that she saw her husband, but she knew he was around by the sound of his distinctive pacing. Knowing he was there and waiting for her made it easier for Marian to call the family together for one last reunion and bid them farewell. The stories that follow are similar to Marian's.

BEDSIDE SHADOWS

Callie was an obese woman who had been in near total dependence on her husband, Charles. It never occurred to her that Charles might die first. When he died suddenly from cardiac arrest, Callie went into shock. Although she survived her husband for five years, it was a borderline survival.

Callie's only discernible goal in life after Charles's death was to join him. She soon became totally dependent on her son, who took her into his home. To the day she died she never forgave him for calling 911 the night she went into respiratory arrest. She was ready to go. Her son's call to the emergency squad frustrated her to no end.

Finally, Callie came closer to her goal. She had become a hospice patient. Soon, we began to hear her talk about Charles and their life together. Then one day Callie noted how she saw Charles at the nursing home. First he was walking past her door. Then he was standing at her door. Later he was sitting in a chair in the corner of her room. The next day Charles came to the side of her bed; he just stood there intermittently for a few days. Finally, one morning he was lying in bed with her: "Just waiting for me," she said. That afternoon Callie and Charles left together.

For Granny (chapter two), it was the vision of her deceased son coming back to build a shed so that she could pack for the journey that lay ahead. For my wife, Dawn, it was a vision of her parents hours before she died: "Mom! Dad! Wait! I'm coming!" For Dawn, as well, it was the "man with the mustache," who drove her nuts because he just sat in a chair in our bedroom. She wanted him to "bring the bus around" so she could get on with the journey. He was the bus driver, and she just wanted him to do his job, to get on the road.

All of the above sightings were experienced by the dying. While this phenomenon is most common, a less commonly reported experience is that of surviving family members seeing the shadows of people who were seen clearly by the dying person.

Rosie had been in a coma for several days. Her mother, Charlene, a woman in her late sixties, kept a long and lonely vigil.

One evening, as Charlene sat quietly at her daughter's bedside, Rosie began to stir and with no further warning sat straight up in her bed. Never expecting her daughter to regain consciousness, Charlene began to entertain the thought that maybe, just maybe, Rosie was going to beat the odds.

Rosie looked at her mother and then pointed at the door to her room and said excitedly, "Look, Mom. They're coming for me!"

Charlene looked, but she didn't see anyone or anything. She turned back to Rosie, and what she saw at that moment would remain with her the rest of her life. Rosie was lying flat in her bed—she had died. At the bedside opposite from where Charlene sat, the shadows of three people hovered over Rosie's body. One at a time the shadows disappeared.

What did Charlene actually see? She claims she saw shadows, the shadows of Rosie's reality. If Marian saw her husband, Granny saw her son, and Dawn saw her parents as well as the bus driver, then we can but assume that there are indeed shadows to be seen somewhere, someplace, by the person who is open to this illusive but illuminating dimension of time, space, and spiritual reality.

REPORTS FROM HISTORY

GUSTAV MAHLER (1860–1911) It has been reported that in 1911, as the German composer Gustav Mahler was spending the last days of his life in a Vienna sanitarium, his sister came to visit, and as she walked into the room Mahler asked, "Who is that strange lady?"

His sister fled the room, fleeing that which she did not understand. Given what we know now, it is possible that Mahler was not speaking of his sister as a "strange lady." Perhaps he had seen someone else in the room that his sister could not see. Apparently no one tried to talk with him about this "strange lady," and we shall never know for sure whom Gustav saw at that moment.

However, we do know that "during his last conscious moments a smiling Mahler was moving his fingers, conducting an 'imaginary' orchestra, and murmuring, 'Little Mozart, Little Mozart.'"[3] Did Mahler actually see the child prodigy Mozart? We do not know, but it is certainly possible.

FREDERIC CHOPIN (1810–1849) A little past midnight on October 17, 1849, the Polish pianist and composer Frederic Chopin awoke shouting, "Mother, my poor mother!" His doctor asked him if he was in pain, and Chopin responded, "No more," and died almost instantly.[4] Did Chopin actually see his deceased mother? Probably.

In this case no one asked Chopin if his mother was saying anything to him or how it felt to have her once again at his bedside. There was so little time between his expressed awareness and his last breath; and that is the way it is sometimes.

SERGE RACHMANINOFF (1873–1943) The Russian pianist and composer Serge Rachmaninoff began what he clearly knew would be his last tour of the United States on February 8, 1943. Soon into the concert tour the pianist of all pianists was stricken with severe illness. He was transported to his home in Beverly Hills, California, where he had previously predicted: "This is my last home on earth. Here I will die."[5]

On the evening of March 28, 1943, Rachmaninoff began the process of slipping away, but as he did so he persisted in trying to convince those at his bedside that music was being played nearby. Just as persistently, they reassured him that there was no music. Finally, Rachmaninoff acquiesced to a compromise and said, "Then it is in my head." Soon after that "admission," one of history's greatest musicians died.

But was the music just in Rachmaninoff's head? Probably not. The chances are great that this dying man was hearing his last symphony on Earth. Perhaps the music was coming from a dimension beyond the pale. If only someone would have asked Serge *what* music was being played. It would be so fascinating and instructive to know *which* composition he was hearing. There is a good chance he might not have been able to identify the score, but could he have intoned the melody? Possibly. But we will never know. The knowledge is forever lost. The energy spent in denying Rachmaninoff's reality in those last moments of his life could well have been used to enjoy that last symphony with the maestro; and all of us, generations later, would be far more enriched and the wiser about death and dying.

PETER ILITCH TCHAIKOVSKY (1840–1893) On November 6, 1893, in St. Petersburg, Russia, Peter Ilitch Tchaikovsky, who only eight days before had conducted the premiere of his *Symphonie Pathetique,* lay on his deathbed suffering from cholera and uttering expressions of what was considered delirium. But in his

final moments Tchaikovsky came out of this supposed psychological state, which had combined with symptoms of physical
suffocation, and suddenly opened his eyes. According to his
brother, Modeste:

> There was an indescribable expression of unclouded
> consciousness. Passing over the others standing in the
> room, he looked at the three nearest him, and then
> toward heaven. There was a certain light for a moment
> in his eyes, which was soon extinguished, at the same
> time with his breath.[6]

What happened? We do not really know, and until we meet
Peter Ilitch in the Great Concert Hall, it will always be a mystery.
But it is clear that something momentous occurred. Though we
are left to speculate, we are sure of one thing: Tchaikovsky saw
something or someone, a vision, a presence that beckoned to him.

ST. MARTIN OF TOURS (C. 316–C. 397) As St. Martin lay on his
deathbed in Candes, France, he composed and performed
a metaphorical opus. Though many had gathered for the
performance, it appears that no one was listening. According to
Sulpicius Severus, an early Christian ascetic and author of *Life
of St. Martin of Tours,* "Martin knew long in advance the time of
his death." As the time suddenly drew near, Martin called his
brother monks to his bedside. As they stood around his room
that day, Martin, with the frankness of those who know they are
dying, informed his community that he would soon be dead.

All who heard this were overcome with grief. In their
sorrow they cried to him with one voice: "Father, why

are you deserting us? Who will care for us when you are gone? Savage wolves will atttack your flock, and who will save us from their bite when our shepherd is struck down? We know you long to be with Christ, but your reward is certain and will not be any less for being delayed. You will do better to show pity for us, rather than forsake us."[7]

According to this account, Martin of Tours broke down and wept. Then, reclaiming some composure, he prayed: "Lord, if your people still need me, I am ready for the task; your will be done." Soon after this prayer, "he saw the devil standing near. 'Why do you stand there, you bloodthirsty brute?' he cried." It was then that Martin "gave up his spirit to heaven."[8]

One way to read the account by Sulpicius Severus, and the more common view to be sure, is that here was a holy man so loved and so terribly needed by his community that he was willing to rise from his deathbed and continue caring for his flock. Indeed, he even had to fend off the Evil One who stalked him in the very midst of his holy brethren. But in the end God intervened and took Martin to his just reward.

Another, and perhaps more accurate, read is that Martin carefully orchestrated a final opus for the sake of the community he had formed at Liguge, France, the community he so dearly loved. He knew that he was dying, and he accepted it. He was looking forward to being with his Lord. He wanted his beloved brothers to be at his side when he publicly debuted this opus, which we might entitle the "Song of Salvation." But sadly, they did not listen.

Instead, this dysfunctionally dependent community could only see their own needs and their own pending loss. They failed to comprehend the courage it took for Martin to tell them that he was dying. They did not hear the subtle plea to "let me go." He needed permission from those he loved to go on to his God. For all we know he never received that permission. Instead, those for whom he had done so much made his departure much more painful than it needed to be.

Whether Martin truly saw the devil is open for debate. It is quite likely, however, that he experienced the work of the devil through the unwitting hands of his beloved brethren, who attempted to hold him in place.

THE SPIRITUAL CONNECTION

Therefore, since we are surrounded by so great a cloud of witnesses, let us rid ourselves of every burden and sin that clings to us and persevere in running the race that lies before us.

HEBREWS 12:1

It is difficult to stand at the bedside of the dying day after day and deny the existence, the truth, the power, and the redeeming grace of the cloud of witnesses. The witnesses seem to put the lie to certain doctrines of faith that declare one organized church, with its exclusionist claims to everlasting life, at an advantage over all others. This cloud of witnesses arrives on the scene whether the dying person is Catholic, Protestant, Jewish, Native American, or none of the above. The witnesses patiently and lovingly assemble whether the awaited one has gone to church daily, weekly, monthly, on Easter and Christmas only, or not at all.

The only apparent membership qualification for joining the Great Cloud of Witnesses is a capacity for love. Perhaps the only hoop we need to jump through in order to establish perpetual residency within the Great Cloud is Jesus' commandment: Love one another as I love you (John 15:12).

Sheila obviously loved her little infant girl and her socially disgraced sister, Elena. But would the child and the sister have returned to Sheila's bedside if they in turn had not loved Sheila? Yet, as Robert Bly suggests, it goes even beyond love to the "third body"—the relationship founded on love:

> *A man and a woman sit near each other . . .*
> *Their breaths together feed someone whom we do not*
> *know . . . They obey a third body that they share in*
> *common.*
> *They have made a promise to love that body.*
>
> ROBERT BLY,
> "THE THIRD BODY"[9]

Marian and her husband ("Dad"), as well as Callie and Charles, surely responded to the Lord's call to "love one another." Their daily response to that call, their triumphs and failures, their commitment and dedication to each other defined something so visible yet unseen: their relationship. And so it was that even the promise that they made to each other on the day of their weddings, to stand by each other through the joys and the sorrows of life until death did them part, was put to the lie as Marian and Callie were dying. In the end we find that even death did not do them part. The relationship, the third body, survived and endured despite physical death. The third body survives death because of the mutually attentive relationship that had been lived out: a habit of listening, caring, nourishing, challenging, embracing, and seeking one another and God.

The relationships between Dawn and her parents, Chopin and his mother, Rachmaninoff and his music endured through the trials of life and the agonies of dying. The strength of those relationships in the end became a transformative, if not transfigurative, presence. Dawn's relationship with her Lord allowed her to see the transfigurative presence of Christ in the "man with the mustache," the bus driver.

The strength of the loving relationship between Charlene and Rosie provided a grace-filled moment as Charlene was able to see the shadows of those who had come for her daughter. It may have been a grace-filled moment, but as Dietrich Bonhoeffer has pointed out, "There is no such thing as cheap grace." [10] The cost for Charlene, Dee, and all others who are left behind at the moment of a loved one's death, includes a premium that is paid in heartache: the painful ripping apart that occurs when we face the fact that what has been will no longer be. The dividend, however, will continue to be received.

QUESTIONS FOR REFLECTION AND DISCUSSION

How would I describe my relationship with my significant other? With my God? With my church?

How will these relationships survive death?

When my time comes, who will step forward from that cloud of witnesses?

CHAPTER FIVE

listening to
the call of the road

*W*hen a hospice patient begins talking about moving, traveling, or getting ready to make a change in whatever way, the hospice team takes immediate note. Such language must not be ignored, denied, challenged, or devalued in any way. The dying person is trying to tell us something vitally important: his or her body is signaling that death is on its way. Indeed, a change of venue is in the offing. It may not happen today or even this week, but it is closing in.

Often such utterances by the dying are either ignored or degraded by those at the bedside. In our efforts to keep our dying loved one "grounded in reality," we run the serious risk of shutting off any further communication with him or her. People who are dying certainly, if only subconsciously, try to inform us of what is real for them right now. Theirs is a reality far different from ours, a vision unlike our own but no less real. The reality of the dying may be even more authentic than what we believe is real.

To listen to the dying as they speak of travel and change is to listen to metaphors for the coming of death. While the dying person may not be able, in a conscious and direct way, to articulate the awareness that death is becoming more imminent, he or she will often communicate through metaphors. The metaphors chosen by the dying are limited only by the boundaries of meaningful human experience. The person may be traveling by plane, train, automobile, horse, or boat. He or she might be packing a suitcase or preparing to move to a "new place." These are just a few metaphors that ease the person—and, if they will listen, loved ones—into one of the most significant changes of life.

In chapter three, Val, the eighty-five-year-old retired truck driver, speaks of "hitting the road," responding to the dispatcher and the "Great Dispatcher," but for her these may have been consciously chosen metaphors. This chapter focuses on the subconscious use of metaphor when, like Harley in chapter two, there seems to be no other way to communicate what needs to be said. It is similar to the way in which physician and poet William Carlos Williams once described his interaction with patients:

> We begin to see that the underlying meaning of all
> they want to tell us . . . is the poem,
> the poem which their lives are being lived to realize . . .
> the poem springs from the half-spoken words . . .[1]

PLANES, TRAINS, AUTOMOBILES, BUSES, BOATS, AND HORSES

The mode of transportation utilized by a person on the way to life beyond is usually in keeping with that person's life experience. The common theme, though, is travel. And once it is time, there is no delay.

"Go get my airline tickets."

Burt was forty years old and had been diagnosed with lung cancer. Surgery was prescribed. Surgery was performed. Surgery was aborted. The cancer was so pervasive that the surgical team closed him back up and returned him to his room.

The breaking of the news to Burt, his thirty-six-year-old wife, Carole, and their two teenage daughters went as well as could be expected. At least they might have as long as six months to prepare for Burt's death and to do some of the things they had dreamed of doing as a family. Burt would be going home in a few days, and they could take it from there.

On a Friday evening three days after the surgery, Denise, a family friend, walked into Burt's hospital room. Denise tried to hide her shock upon seeing the dramatic physical deterioration of a strong and vital man. In the middle of their conversation, Burt blurted out a special request to Denise: "Do you think you could run over to the airport to pick up my tickets? If you could, I would sure appreciate it."

Taken a bit by surprise, Denise responded, "Well . . . sure. I didn't know you had a trip planned." She glanced at Carole and saw that she was just as confused.

"When do you plan to travel, Burt?" Denise asked.

"Where do you think you're going?" Carole wanted to know.

"Soon," a very weak Burt replied. He drifted off to sleep. Carole looked at Denise and motioned toward the door.

As they walked the hallway together, Carole said, "Now I don't have a clue what that whole business about the airline tickets means. First of all, if he has a trip scheduled for the company, and he doesn't, the tickets will be delivered to him. The fact is the only trip he has scheduled right now is to go home Monday morning."

"It's probably the medication he's on and the anesthesia they gave him the other day." Denise was trying to be reassuring.

The next day, Saturday, Burt's recovery seemed to slip. He was weaker, his blood pressure had dipped, and he was having fewer moments of responsiveness. "Just leave me alone!" he commanded—whether it was to a nurse or to Carole.

Carole and the children went to early worship service on Sunday morning and then went directly from church to the hospital. Burt had experienced a restful night. He had eaten well from the breakfast tray, and he looked stronger. The old Burt was coming back. Carole was elated at what she saw and heard—at least for a brief moment.

"Go get my airline tickets," Burt said to no one in particular.

"But Honey, you have no trip planned."

"Yes I do! Please, for God's sake, go get my tickets!"

"Okay, okay, okay!" said Carole. "Later."

"No, now! Please, all of you. Go now. Right now. Just go!"

Carole reassured him, "Okay, Honey. We'll be back. You get some rest."

While they had planned to go to a restaurant for Sunday brunch, Carole suggested they go down to the hospital cafeteria instead. They needed to talk about how best to handle this persistent issue of the airline tickets. It must be a hallucination. He would get through it, and so would they.

Deciding that it was best to placate Burt, the family headed back to his room. As they stepped off the elevator, the charge nurse rushed over from the nurses' station. "We didn't realize you were still here. We tried calling you at home. We just found him ten minutes ago. I'm so terribly sorry."

So it was that Burt got his airline tickets.

"I hear the train coming!"
On top of dealing with a lifelong diabetic condition, Clint had battled cancer for seven of his seventy-two years and congestive heart failure for three of those years. He had done all that medical science and technology had to offer. Now he had decided to do no more. Verleen, on the other hand, seemed to be somewhere else. When I called to arrange a time to meet with them, she sounded guarded and tentative.

I soon discovered that Clint loved to tell tales of life on the railroad, tales that took me to some of the places he had been and introduced me to a few of the people he had met while riding the rails. He relived a number of crises he had encountered and soon became lost in the memory of how he and Verleen had met. He laughed now at what was hardly laughable at the time: her parents' strenuous objections to her marrying a "railroading roustabout." Then, at a rare moment when Verleen was not in the room, Clint confessed, "I'm just tired of all this. I can't seem to talk with Verleen about it. I mean she just won't let me begin or even get close to the topic of my dying."

The next day, Clint was in the hospital. He had experienced severe breathing difficulty, and Verleen dialed 911. She requested that I call her at the hospital.

"I panicked," Verleen admitted. "I know he's dying, but I hate so much to even say it. Clint's reaction last night when they brought him here has convinced me that this is real. He wants absolutely nothing more done, nothing. I must respect that. He just asked if you could come up. He wants to see you."

Later that day I arrived in Clint's hospital room at a time when Verleen and their son were meeting with the funeral director to make early arrangements. I entered the room as two nurses were leaving. Clint was sitting up in bed.

"What are you doing in here?" I asked jokingly.

"Ron, I'm dying," said Clint.

As if they had rehearsed it, both nurses, in unison, countered Clint's revealed truth with a contrived falsehood: "Oh, Clint, you're not going to die!"

I simply asked, "How does that feel, Clint?"

Without the slightest hesitation, Clint said, "Free, Ron, free! I have never felt so free."

He went on to note that Verleen had finally accepted that he was dying. Now they could talk about it together. Clint had a sense of being set free from something that had "felt like a prison—like solitary confinement." Clint cried as he admitted to this feeling of having been pardoned for a crime he did not commit.

At about 10:00 P.M., my pager went off. It was Verleen, wanting me to call her right back. She thanked me for going up to see Clint that afternoon. She was sorry to have missed my visit. "Clint so appreciates your coming. He told me you asked him how it feels and he said he feels free. But that is not the reason I called. Something has happened that I'm not sure I understand."

"What has happened?" I could hear Verleen crying.

"Well, Ron, it's this: Clint has been in the hospital probably fifty times in the last seven years. Never once did he ever—I mean ever—call me from the hospital. Fifteen minutes ago he called me. He said he just wanted to wish me a good night; and then . . . and then he told me he loved me. I can count on one hand the number of times he told me he loved me: when I agreed to marry him, our wedding night, and then right after our son was born—three times in fifty-two years of knowing the man! Well, make it four times now."

"Wow, Verleen. How do you feel about that call?"

"To be frank, I feel loved on the one hand and cautiously confused on the other."

"Cautiously confused? How do you mean that?"

"What I mean is this: If he is really in his right mind, I feel loved and so grateful. But if he doesn't know what he is saying . . . "

"Why do you even raise the question?" I wondered if there were some deeply unresolved issues in this marriage.

"Again, to be perfectly frank, I'm afraid the cancer has gone to his brain. The very last thing he said was: 'I hear the train coming. It's time to go, Verleen. Good-bye.' Come to think of it, that's what he said. He didn't say good night; he said good-bye. I just don't know what to make of it."

I was not quite sure what it all meant either. At the risk of sounding really stupid, I proceeded to hazard a guess. It seemed to me that Clint was getting ready to depart, and that there was something very important he wanted Verleen to know.

Early the next morning, Verleen received a call from the hospital. Clint's train had arrived.

"It's a big black beautiful car."
It is evening and, although I don't yet know it, less than one week before Dawn, my wife, will die. Dawn is insisting that I help her get out of bed.

"Why?" I ask. "What's up?"

"I need to go. Just get me out of this bed," she insists.

"But where are you going?"

No answer, but she is pulling herself to the edge of the bed and trying to scale the bed rails. I decide to go with the flow and lower the rails.

This person who loved to climb trees tries to raise herself to a sitting position, but she has no strength to get there. Even with the assistance of my hand, she has barely enough power to pull herself upward. Sitting on the edge of the bed is clearly an uncertain project for her. She is unable to remain upright on her own, so I sit down beside her with my arm around her shoulder. *My God,* I think to myself, *there is so little to hold anymore! All that is left is her determined spirit.*

"I need you, Ron. I need you to get me over there." Dawn points to the dresser some six feet from where we sit.

"Why?"

"Because I will be able to see it from there."

"See what?"

There is no response.

"Dawn, we are at a point where you have almost no strength. You can't raise yourself out of bed. You can't stand alone. You can't walk anymore, even with assistance. If I were not holding you, you could not even be sitting here."

"I know, Ron, but get me over there. Carry me if you have to. Please. Then I will be able to see it."

"Okay, here goes, but I hope you can tell me what 'it' is when we get there."

Once I'm standing at the dresser, with Dawn in my arms, she tells me to stand her up on the floor. "Hold me up, Ron. There. Don't you see it?" she asks excitedly.

"No, Babe. Your vision is different from mine these days. You need to tell me what you see. Can you do that?"

"It's a car, Ron. A big, black beautiful car. I wish you could see it. It will come for you too, sometime; then you will see it."

Feeling exasperated by her demands to do things she cannot do, frustrated by lack of sleep due to her late-night forays into a world I cannot fathom, and demoralized by the sight of a once vital human being reduced to a skeleton, I am now just a little spooked. While I cannot see what she sees, I know that what she does see is within my reach but untouchable. Dawn is right. One day that big, black beautiful car will come for me, and then I will see it. Dawn has found another way to tell me that it is time for her to go.

"Hitch them up—it's time to go."
Duncan and Marilou had spent their entire sixty-year marriage on their farm along the Nishnabotna River in southwest Iowa. They had raised their four children there. They had managed a prosperous farming operation, first using horses to plant and

harvest crops, then advancing to tractors and combines, and in later years leasing the land to a young farmer.

Duncan was dying from emphysema, a malady he mostly acquired from breathing the dusty conditions of the farmland, harvesting the crops, and raising hogs in confinement. He was a realist and claimed to know what had caused his decline in health. He had made a living on the farm, and he was prepared to make a dying on it as well: "Living and dying are of a piece." Duncan was also a philosopher.

"Dunk," as he liked to be called by his friends, was a man of purpose. When it was time to plant, it was time to plant! Nothing and no one would stand in the way of planting the crops. It did not matter what was scheduled or how long ago the date had been set. If the conditions were right for planting, everything else would take a backseat. Similarly, nothing and no one would interfere with harvesting the crops. According to a friend and neighbor, "Plenty of plans got dunked by Dunk over the years."

When Dunk realized he had a serious health problem, predictably, his attention turned toward curing the disease. Everything else took second place to getting well. When it became clear that there would be no cure, Dunk gave priority to "making the best out of what the Lord has given me."

So it should have been no surprise to anyone that when Dunk's physician gave him a six-months-or-less prognosis, Dunk's only response was: "Then I've got some things to do." Upon returning home, he methodically arranged his affairs and made sure that Marilou knew every detail.

One evening as Marilou was tidying up his hospital bed in their living room, Dunk said to her, "Hitch them up." Thinking he meant the blankets that were down to his hips, she pulled them up to his shoulders.

"There. Is that okay now?"

"Didn't you hear me?" Dunk's tone of consternation took Marilou by surprise.

"What do you mean? You want the blankets up over your head?"

"What the hell are *you* talking about? I said hitch them up!"

"Hitch what up? I thought you meant the blankets. So what do you want hitched up?"

"The horses, for God's sake. The horses. Hitch them up!"

"Now you just listen here, Duncan. There aren't any horses to hitch up. You sold them years ago. Remember?"

"Good God, woman, don't you see them?"

"No, I don't. There are no horses around here."

"Marilou, you've got to understand. Look out the window. The horses are looking in the window. I can see them. They've come for me. It's time to go. Hitch them up."

Frustrated to the hilt, Marilou decided that it wasn't worth getting into an argument at this point. "Whatever you say, Duncan, but I have to get to the bathroom. When I get back we'll talk about hitching up your horses. In the meantime, just hold your horses."

Upon her return, Marilou found him sound asleep. His breathing was shallow, and at times he seemed to hold his breath for several seconds. But at least he was asleep and off his kick about hitching up his imaginary horses. Deciding that this was a good time to go to bed herself, Marilou headed for the bedroom just off the living room. On her way, she decided to look out the window where Duncan claimed he could see horses gazing into the house. As expected, Marilou saw nothing but the dark of night. "Yet there was this feeling, this sense that we were not alone," she told me later.

At about 3:00 A.M., Marilou thought she heard Duncan cry out for her. Crawling out of bed, she realized that whatever she had heard was different from anything she had ever heard from Dunk before. "Duncan, what do you want? I'll be right there." But there was no answer. As she stood at his bedside, she could clearly see that somehow the horses had gotten hitched up. They had surely come for their master.

"They've given me a ticket for the bus."
She seems unusually agitated, depressed, and ill at ease. Her countenance is the all-too-familiar feature I have come to know and fear: the furrowed brow, the dark and haunted look in her eyes. Normally, Dawn's excitement about life is like a house full of enthusiastic friends and relatives welcoming home a long absent loved one. When she is up, she is like that house: fully lit, curtains open, music playing, and laughter ringing through the rafters, infusing the neighborhood with joy. When she is down, she is like a dark and haunted house. Despair, defeat, and disaster hang everywhere. The heaviness of the air weighs down on my spirit like an elephant standing on my chest. Sometimes the moods of depression last for days, even a couple of weeks; but we do not have that kind of time anymore. I begin to feel a certain low-grade panic.

The fact is, in the thirty-five years we have been together, I have had little luck pulling Dawn out of the pits of despair. In the end she has always been the one to pull herself out. *Is this the way it will end?* I ask myself. *Is she going to die in the midst of her hell on Earth, a hell of being trapped within herself?*

"You seem depressed, Babe," I say.

"Hub, I just don't know how to get from here to there," she says with both hands raised as if she were beseeching the gods to open the heavens and display the answer to her question in neon lights.

I think I know what she means, but I had better ask: "From here to where?"

At this point she looks at me as if I were totally addled and hopelessly senseless. "Heaven, Ron! Where else?"

Well, I know one thing, and that is the simple fact that I don't really know the answer. I know all the tried and trite answers: Jesus is the way. Trust in the Lord. You have it made. Don't worry, be happy. Go with the flow. Let go and let God. But something tells me that none of that is going to sell; at least this customer won't buy it.

I sit on the edge of the bed and take her hand in mine. "I don't know either. But I do know one thing, Dawn: you will figure it out, the answer will come to you. You have always been an expert at figuring things out, and you will figure this out as well. Maybe we should pray together on this one."

So we pray for the Lord to show Dawn "how to get from here to the Great There." At the end of our prayer, Dawn adds, "Lord, show me soon. I want to go now, please."

The next morning she is still in a depressed mood, barely responding to me. She just does not want to talk, and I know better than to press the issue. Having freshened her up and given her a liquid breakfast, I kiss her good-bye and head for work. A friend will be along to sit with her until I come home for lunch. "I will see you later, Dawnie. I love you."

"I love you too" would be her normal response. This time it is a deadening, deafening, haunting silence. All I can think about while I'm at work is the despairing scene in my own bedroom of my soul mate trapped in her chamber of silence. I feel so completely helpless, as helpless as I have ever felt in my life.

When I arrive home I can hear Dawn's voice even before I open the front door. She is singing. Her voice is light and carefree.

"You seem so happy, Dawn. When I left for work you were so down, and now you seem so up. It is so good to see you this way. What's going on?"

"Oh, Ron! Those people who have been hanging around here have given me a ticket for the bus and have invited me to go with them," she exclaims. A glorious transformation has occurred. What appeared to be doom itself has now become the very embodiment of hope.

Reasonably certain that I know where the bus is going, I still think it best to ask, "What is the bus's destination?"

"Well, heaven, of course!"

Previously, these people had been ever present in the room, but Dawn did not know who they were. She was not even sure whether they were male or female. They never talked to her or to one another. She was not sure why they were even there, but there they were, sitting and waiting. Today, however, they not only offered her a ticket for the bus, but they revealed their identities. Among the people on the bus are Dawn's parents, a deceased friend named Bill, Dawn's grandparents, and others. She knows now how she will "get from here to there"—and she knows she will not be making the trip alone.

Sailing to the distant shore

At 605 Third Street in Council Bluffs, Iowa, a huge fourteen-room, three-story Victorian mansion sits on a high terrace along one of the bluffs for which the city is named. From the mansion's front door one can see much of the city. Above the housetops and church steeples the westward view carries the eye beyond the Missouri River to the city of Omaha, Nebraska.

Grenville M. Dodge, brigadier general of Union volunteers during the American Civil War and chief construction engineer of the Union Pacific Railroad, built this home in 1869 for his wife, Ruth Anne, and their two daughters, Anne and Eleanor. Today the mansion is a public museum and a national historic landmark.

The Dodge House is the scene for much beauty and joy, especially during the Christmas season, when the museum sponsors the annual Christmas Tree Festival. With an elaborately decorated tree in each room, the Dodge House resonates with the message of hope.

On September 4, 1916, the atmosphere was anything but festive at the home of Grenville and Ruth Anne Dodge. Ruth Anne was dying.

On the evening of September 2, Ruth Anne, sitting up in her bed, informed her family that she had just been on a rocky shore. Through the mist along this shore she had seen a boat approaching. In the prow of the boat a beautiful woman, an angel, carried a small bowl under one arm, extending the other arm outright toward Ruth Anne. The angelic woman unmistakably invited Ruth Anne to "partake of the water flowing from the vessel."

On the evenings of September 3 and 4, the boat returned with the beautiful young woman, her vessel of water, and her invitation to the dying Mrs. Dodge. Each time, the angel spoke twice, saying: "Drink. I bring you both a promise and a blessing." It was after the third visit that Ruth Anne reported to her daughter Anne that she had consumed the water and had experienced the feeling of being "transformed into a new and glorious spiritual being." Ruth Anne Dodge died shortly thereafter.

Anne and Eleanor affirmed their mother's experience of seeing the boat, the angel, and hearing the angel speak to her. Apparently the two young women were able to dialogue with their dying mother, perhaps enabling her to finally partake of the proffered water. They listened and learned.

In 1917, Ruth Anne Dodge's daughters memorialized the life of their mother and etched the symbolic language of the dying on the social conscience of a community. It was then that the daughters commissioned the sculptor Daniel Chester French (1850–1931) to create a statue that would represent their mother's angel standing in the prow of a boat, holding a vessel of water.

The statue, cast in solid bronze and mounted on a granite base, was dedicated in 1920. It sits on a bluff about half a mile away from the family home. The Black Angel, as the statue has come to be known, resides on the edge of Fairview Cemetery. The larger-than-life figure stands with her wings closed, her right arm outstretched, and a vessel of streaming water held in her left hand.

Daniel Chester French, who was also the sculptor of the seated Abraham Lincoln in the Lincoln Memorial in Washington, D.C., as well as the Standing Lincoln in the state capitol building in Lincoln, Nebraska, is reported to have claimed the Black Angel as one of his very best achievements.

It certainly stands as a monument to the wonders of listening to the language of the dying.[2]

PACKING IT UP

Granny (chapter two) informed her family that she had seen her deceased son, who was building a shed for her things. Granny was trying to tell her family that she needed to pack up and go on to her God. The stories that follow here present further evidence that there is poetry to be heard in the voices of the dying.

"Pack my suitcase."

Delores, a ninety-eight year old dying of "declining health status" (old age) and a resident of the care center for nearly ten years, told her daughter, "pack my suitcase." Her daughter whispered this information to me as I walked into the room, adding, "But she has no suitcase. What's going on?"

"Well, I can't be sure, but I suspect your mother is trying to tell us that she knows her time is short. She is getting ready to pack it all up and go on to her God."

"That may be," says the daughter, "but she doesn't look any different today than she has for weeks, months even."

Delores died early the next morning. We can only presume that she got her suitcase packed for the trip.

"I'm getting me a different place."

Frank was a crotchety eighty-eight-year-old farmer dying of congestive heart failure. He also suffered from the heartache of having to sell his farm and move into the city to live with his daughter and her family. There appeared to be only three things that Frank had brought with him to the city from the farmstead: his bed, his easy chair, and his god-awful cigars!

I visited Frank every Friday, and I swear you could smell the cigars a block away. On this particular Friday, I knew from all previous Fridays that Frank would be sitting in his easy chair. The haze of cigar smoke would fill the room, my lungs, and every thread of my clothes. As usual, Frank would greet me and express his pleasure in seeing me again. It was always fun trying to predict what his chief gripe of the week would be. Usually Frank would be disturbed about something the president or Congress or the courts had done or should have done. Once in a while Frank would aim his consternation at his daughter, Frannie.

To my surprise, Frank was not smoking a cigar, nor did he have any complaints. On the surface he seemed like the same old Frank: same old corduroy bib overalls, same old black wool sweater underneath, same leather slippers from antiquity. But there was something different today. Maybe it was just the absence of smoke from that old rotten rope that Frank called a cigar.

No, it was more than the breathable air. As the visit progressed, I came to realize that he was just plain different today— but an indefinable different. He was more reflective without openly sharing any rich insights. He was just letting things be without finding fault with the world around him.

As I was leaving, I said, "Well, Frank, I'll see you next Friday."

Reaching for the cigar box and pulling out the one and only cigar, he lit it and said, "Think I'll have my last cigar on you, Ron."

Frannie piped in at that point: "I'm going down to the drug-store in a few minutes. I'll pick up some more cigars for you."

"Nah, that won't be necessary. I'm givin' them up. Don't taste like they used to, anyway. They don't know how to make cigars these days; might as well smoke cardboard!"

Now that's the old Frank, I thought.

"By the way, Ron, I won't be here next Friday," said Frank, very matter-of-fact.

"Oh really? What's happening?"

"Well, I'll tell ya. I'm coming into some money. Should get the check today or tomorrow. Then, I'm getting me a different place."

I glanced at Frannie and could see that all of this was news to her. She started to respond to him, but I interrupted: "Well, Frank, you just let me know where you are, and you take care." I motioned to Frannie to join me outside, and we left Frank to his cigar.

"What's that all about?" she asked. "He isn't getting any money in the mail. He isn't going anywhere."

"I'm not at all sure, but don't argue with him. I think he's trying to tell us that his time is near, that he's going to be leaving us soon. When, I don't know."

That was Frank's last cigar, the last day he sat in his favorite chair, and his last Friday. That was the last time I saw Frank. He got himself a different place early Sunday morning.

"They're offering me a larger room."

"I think I will," she said to no one in particular, at least no one I could see.

"You think you will what?" I was readying a pan of water to give her a sponge bath.

"Oh, I think I'll take them up on their offer."

"What offer? Whose offer?"

"Those people," she replied as if I should know.

The strange thing is, I did know. I knew it was those people just as well as I knew that rainbows follow sunshine in the midst of a rainstorm. They were the ones Dawn talked about so frequently: the folks who were increasingly present around her bed, in the hallway, and on the bus. They were people I could not see, but people we both knew were deceased.

"So what kind of offer is it?" I asked.

"Just wheel me down the hall. Then knock on the second door to the right, and you will see." Dawn told me this as if she were a little girl asking for help unwrapping a Christmas gift, knowing full well that what lies inside is the very thing she longs for most.

"Well, Babe, I can't do that. This bed is too heavy and unwieldy. We'll need more help. Maybe tomorrow." That seemed to satisfy her. "But tell me, what are those people offering to you?"

"Oh, Ron, you won't believe this, but they're offering me a larger room. It's going to be beautiful. I can't wait for you to see it!"

Five days later Dawn found her way into the larger room.

THE SPIRITUAL CONNECTION

Then Moses stretched out his hand over the sea, and the LORD swept the sea with a strong east wind throughout the night and so turned it into dry land. When the water was thus divided, the Israelites marched into the midst of the sea on dry land, with the water like a wall to their right and to their left.

EXODUS 14:21–22

Each one of the stories recounted in this chapter is an exodus event with no exception, whether it was
- Burt pleading for his airline tickets
- Clint hearing the train coming
- Dawn needing to see the car, or excitedly catching the bus
- Duncan demanding that the horses be hitched up
- Delores requesting that her suitcases be packed

These are accounts of people at the end of life preparing for a new life. They are tales of ordinary people having extraordinary experiences. If the Spirit of God speaks to us through human experience, then there is no event of God more profound than that which occurs at the end of one's life.

That same Spirit and a similar event of God are available to those of us who stand the vigil and listen well to the language of the dying. We stand on holy ground at such times, and if we listen to the "strong east wind" of the dying, we will experience something of the glory of God. Perhaps we, too, will be moved to join Moses and the Israelites in singing this song to the Lord:

I will sing to the LORD, for he is gloriously triumphant;
horse and chariot he has cast into the sea.

EXODUS 15:1

To listen to the dying speak of traveling and of moving to a different place is to learn many things:

- Death is not the end
- Our loved one is not and will not be alone
- Moving from here to there is not frightening
- There are a variety of modes of transport available to us as well when our turn comes

No matter what the circumstances may be, dying is an exodus event, a God event, where the "strong east wind" clears the path for the journey to the other side.

In my Father's house there are many dwelling places;
otherwise, how could I have told you
that I am going to prepare a place for you?
And if I go to prepare a place for you,
I will come back again and take you to myself,
so that where I am you also may be.
Where [I] am going you know the way.

JOHN 14:2–4

Frank's sensing he was about to get another place and Dawn's receiving an invitation to move into a larger room are but two examples of people at the end of life experiencing John 14 in a special way. One could argue that because Dawn was very tuned in to Scripture she was simply relating to a very meaningful passage in a conscious and deliberate manner. However, her expressed sense of the larger room being just "down the hall," along with the mystic realities of the unseen others, belie the notion of deliberate thought.

One could hardly attempt the same argument with Frank's experience. Frank was barely conversant with Scripture. His religious practices were minimal throughout his life. No, there was something else going on here. Was it not the symbolic language of the dying meshing with and merging into sacred Scripture? As Elisabeth Kübler-Ross has noted: "The Scriptures are full of symbolic language. If people would listen more to their own intuitive spiritual quadrant . . . they would begin to comprehend the beautiful symbolic language that dying patients use when they try to convey to us their needs, their knowledge, and their awareness."[3]

QUESTIONS FOR REFLECTION AND DISCUSSION

What do I need to do to prepare for my exodus journey?

What will that "special dwelling place" be like?

When my time comes, what mode of transportation will I most likely use to get there?

CHAPTER SIX

❧

hearing the call to forgiveness

*a*ccording to Hannah Arendt, forgiveness, is what got Jesus of Nazareth into trouble.[1] It was not so much his call to "love one another" or even his being perceived as a threat to the established political and ecclesial orders of the time. It was his simple yet complicated call to tolerance and reconciliation that could not be allowed to stand. In a culture where all the answers were in, the social order was clear, good and bad were sharply defined, and right and wrong were religiously delineated, these strange messages to turn the other cheek, to stop by the wayside to help the very enemy of our class, and to pray to God to forgive our sins as we have forgiven others could not be allowed to carry on.

In the end it was Jesus' teachings on forgiveness and reconciliation that led him back to the Father. Even as he hung on the cross, he continued to bear witness to the power of forgiveness: "Father, forgive them, they know not what they do" (Luke 23:34). Having preached the gospel of tolerance, established right order in the world, and suffered persecution for his teachings, Jesus heeded the call to go home to his God.

Similarly, it seems that most people reaching the end of life realize a call to make things right with the significant others in their lives. The need that arises during the last days and weeks of one's life to reconcile differences, to right wrongs and heal hurts, appears to be an unspoken acknowledgement of Christ's teaching. It is by forgiving that we, too, return to our God. In the end, our ability to enter the kingdom may hinge on our willingness to hang on our own cross and plead with our God to "forgive them, for they do not know what they have done; forgive me for my own failures."

Why is it that those who have spent little time in life overtly acknowledging the presence of God begin to do so when mortality looms on their horizon or sits at their door? Why do old hurts that have been retained throughout life loosen their grip on us as life turns to shades of death? Is it because of what John Tarrant describes as the "spiritual opening"?[2] Surely, to come face-to-face with one's own mortality is to encounter a sober moment. For most of us most of the time, such moments are truly spiritual openings.

While experiencing a heightened need to reconcile with others and with their God, many of those who are dying also realize a diminished ability to articulate that need. As we shall see later in this chapter, Alvin Straight, having learned of his own life-threatening diagnosis and that of his estranged brother, set out on a conscious and rigorous journey to realign their relationship.[3] Alvin drove a lawn tractor 280 miles into a spiritual opening. With extraordinary effort and determination, he was able to publicly express his goal and carry out his mission.

As we have seen, others come to realize the same need as Alvin did, but do so later on in the process of dying, at a time when the only apparent way for them to express the event of their "spiritual opening" is through the use of metaphorical language. Clint's first and last call to Verleen from the hospital (chapter five) can be seen as his effort to make things right between them. He wanted her to know that he loved her before he got on his train. When Harley urged his troubled son (chapter two) to "keep hammering on the wall," he was doing more than trying to persuade his son to not take his own life. Mick had suffered the pain of believing his dad had devalued him since the debilitating accident; but now Mick knew for sure that Harley truly loved him.

The stories told here cover a vast landscape of spiritual openings. Most of the instances related involve the use of a symbolic language; others involve conscious and deliberate reconciling behavior. All of the stories recounted here come from the lives of ordinary people who experienced extraordinary spiritual openings for themselves and for the others in their lives. These events of God happened because people listened to a call to forgiveness, a call that they couldn't help following.

GOING AROUND ON THE CAROUSEL

As I inform the charge nurse at the nurses' station that I am here to see Carl, a woman standing nearby says, "Oh, you must be the hospice chaplain. I am Kathryn, Carl's stepdaughter. Actually, he is more like a real dad. The only dad I ever really knew was Carl, and he treated my sister the same way. We never felt anything but love from him. He has always been there for us. He adopted us when he married our mom. Mom told me once that Dad told her he didn't want to refer to us as his stepdaughters; he wanted to be able to say, 'These are my daughters.' That's the kind of man you're about to meet. His first concern always is for others. He never complains. He just takes life as it comes. He loved our mom dearly, always at her beck and call. He took her death so hard. He hasn't been the same since. His health just went down and down after we buried her. In lots of ways he has been a lost soul since Mom died. He keeps talking about wanting to be with her, to see her again, that he has lived a good life, that he is ready to go. Yet I think there's something that's holding him back. We thought he would have died before now, but he's still here. I don't know what it is. Maybe, despite his strong religious beliefs, he is afraid of something. He says he's not afraid. He says he's ready, but I wonder if there isn't something. What do you think?"

"Think?" After this nonstop, unrelenting discourse, I feel numb. Kathryn is a large but not excessively stocky person. She has short blondish hair and looks as if she just stepped out of the beautician's shop. She wears jewelry like she uses words, profusely: large dangling earrings, what appear to be at least three necklaces artfully interwoven, a bracelet on each wrist, and a ring on each finger.

I come out of my stupor. "Well, I think we need to talk to Carl. Would you introduce me to him? We may or may not get anywhere. Sometimes people hang on, as you say, just because they are not ready to go. Not because of any fear or concern that is holding them back; they are just not yet ready, or the Lord isn't ready. We'll see."

Carl is a wizened version of a human being. His complexion is dark, and what little skin remains upon the frame of his body hangs like ripples in a stream. The picture on the wall shouts out to the world what devastation cancer has wrought upon this man. The Carl in that photo is a huge individual, probably weighing about 250 pounds, a healthy version of this man before me who I doubt weighs more than seventy. In the photo Carl looks out at the world with eyes that are filled with joy and love for life. In this bed is a man looking inwardly with troubled eyes, sad eyes, the eyes of an aged and infirm beagle.

He talks about his work as a farm-implement sales representative, of being on the farm as a child and a young man, of his marriage to Helen, and of the unlimited goodness in his life. Tears come to his eyes as he talks about Helen caring for him and how they both thought he would die first. "But the Lord had different plans, I guess," he concludes with an air of resignation. Kathryn is sobbing quietly off to the side, out of Carl's line of vision.

As Carl continues to engage in his life review, he also grows weary. His eyes become heavy, and he begins to drift into sleep. "Carl, I think we are wearing you out," I say.

"No, not at all," he says with a wink. "Just give me a few minutes. I'll be right back."

A few minutes later Carl opens his eyes and looks directly at me. "If you're ready to pray, I am."

"Sure am. What would you like to pray for today?"

"That the Lord take good care of my girls," he says, reaching out once again for his daughter's hand. "And that Freddie and I can go around on the carousel."

I glance over at Kathryn. There's a rather shocked look on her face.

"What carousel? What do you mean, Dad?"

Carl does not respond. He has drifted off to sleep again.

"Who is Freddie?" I ask quietly.

"Dad's son by his first, and very brief, marriage. We have never seen much of Freddie, and neither has Dad. I think it's always been hard for Dad and probably equally hard for Fred as well. After all, while Dad doted on the two daughters that were not his own, he had so little to do with Fred, his own son. That has to be difficult to understand and accept. But that's the way it was; that's the way it had to be, I guess, given the situation with Freddie's mother."

"So, Carl, you and Freddie need to go around on the carousel?" I ask, hoping to garner some definition of intent. Carl does not respond.

My prayers that afternoon speak directly to Carl's request: that the Lord will continue looking after Carl's girls; that he and Freddie can go around on the carousel together. He is asleep as Kathryn and I walk out of the room. "What do you think he means about the carousel?" she asks.

"I was hoping you would have some insight on that yourself, Kathryn. But here's a guess: First of all, it is very common for people reaching the end of life to express a readiness to travel. Some talk about taking a bus, catching a plane, or packing a suitcase. Carl's choice of a carousel may be his way of letting us know that he will be leaving us soon. I think, however, that there is much more going on here. A carousel doesn't really go anywhere; it just goes around and around in the same spot. Carl seems to be saying that he and Freddie need to go around and around together, and I think this expressed need is one we should pay attention to. Is it possible to call Freddie? If he could come here that would be great. But if he could just talk with his father on the phone, that may be all that is needed. Carl has a very important need to relate one last time to his son; I think that is very clear."

As Kathryn and I walk down the hall, she says, "I must call Freddie now. But there's no phone in Dad's room." She takes out her cell phone. "I will call Freddie and arrange a time when I can be here with the cell phone, and he and Dad can talk. That will work."

The next afternoon, Freddie calls. Freddie and his father go around on the carousel. It is a good day for Carl. He is unusually alert. For nearly an hour, father and son talk. Carl asks his son to forgive him for failing to be the dad Freddie deserved. Freddie, taking advantage of this spiritual opening, begs forgiveness for not being more attentive to his father.

Forty-eight hours later, Carl died a peaceful death.

PEACE WITH OTHERS[4]

Steffen's family was at the end of their rope. They were trying to care for him with the assistance of our hospice team, but his anger was so sharp and raw, so intense and total, that they were ready to give up. His mother had requested a meeting with our care team.

Steffen had already denied any chaplain services; therefore, I had not yet encountered this thirty-two year old who was dying of AIDS. I decided, however, to sit in on the conference. As Steffen's mother related her anguish, I asked if she thought he would be open now to a chaplain visit. She replied, "If you call on the phone, be ready to have the phone melt in your ear. But if you want to risk it, try coming with the nurse." Steffen had already "fired" one of our nurses for using the "*A* word," but I decided to take his mother's advice and accompany Steffen's new nurse.

As we exited the car, we could hear Steffen yelling at his mother. I walked in behind the nurse, introduced myself, and sat at a safe distance while the nurse worked with Steffen. As she finished her assessment, I began to talk gently with Steffen, but all of a sudden he began to gag on the phlegm in his throat. I got up, went over to his bedside, and held the bucket for him. That was the beginning of our relationship.

"Thanks, Chaplain. You know, not many people would do what you just did."

"What do you mean, Steffen?"

"I mean even members of my own family are afraid that if they touch that bucket, they'll get it too."

"AIDS?"

"Yeah, damn it," he snapped back with the anger we heard from the driveway. "I'm a leper, man. A goddamned leper."

"You seem to be rather angry, Steffen."

"You're very perceptive, Chaplain."

"Where is that anger coming from? Where is it going?"

"It is coming from the fact that all of the people who I thought were my friends, including my father, have abandoned me." Tears began to form around the corners of Steffen's eyes.

I handed him a tissue and asked, "How have they abandoned you?"

"Well, first of all, I never intended to die this young. I certainly never intended to die here. I wanted to get as far away as possible, and stay away. San Francisco became my home. I only came back here to visit. But now here I am, and I will never leave. Will any of my friends come to see me now that I have AIDS? Hell no. I've called them. I've done everything except plead with them to come. If I had the money, I would pay them to come, for Christ's sake."

"You mentioned your father as one of those who have abandoned you."

"Yeah, he hardly recognizes I'm here. A few days ago, he came home from work and went into their bedroom. Mom was at work. I went in and lay down with him to talk, but he was too tired. So I left. Later, when Mom came home, I overheard him tell her that he had stripped their bed because I had lain in it. I told you, Chaplain, I am a goddamned leper in my own home."

"How does that feel?"

"Like I'm a nonperson. I'm a disease. Look, I know I've been a disappointment to my parents and to my brother and sister. I know what I've done. I've screwed up my life and everybody else's as well, but I can't go back and change it. What is done is done and I'm the one who has done it."

"So, Steffen, where do you go from here? What is all of this saying to you?"

This young man, who had not seen the inside of a church in years and who did not have much of a religious background, looked at me and said, "Chaplain, I think I have a lot of forgiving to do. Will you pray with me?"

As we prayed the Lord's Prayer, tears ran down Steffen's cheek. Moments later he admitted, "I didn't think I would know how to pray that prayer—it's been so long."

"Steffen, you may not have noticed, but you were leading the prayer."

Steffen wept and wept and wept, drying his tears with his pillow, muffling his cries with it as well.

"You said you have a lot of forgiving to do. How is that going to happen?"

"I don't really know, but I'll figure it out. Right now, I feel wrung out. I need to get some sleep. Could you come back next week sometime?"

We agreed that I would return on the same day the following week, but early the following morning Steffen called and asked if I could come right away. "I have a lot to talk to you about before I do what I have to do."

Steffen looked far more energized that morning than when I left him the day before. He told me that he wanted to talk out some of his fears and concerns about asking forgiveness. What if no one wanted to forgive him? What if no one would accept his forgiveness?

We explored Steffen's past experience with forgiveness. He remembered that, as a child, he was the one most likely to seek forgiveness. It was Steffen who tried to heal the wounds of family squabbles. He knew well from experience that sometimes the quest for forgiveness succeeds, and sometimes it does not realize the goal of healing.

"Steffen, why do you even suggest that this is something you need to do?"

"Because . . . because I have to do it."

"In other words, you cannot live with yourself unless you try? And you cannot die without having tried to heal the hurts?"

"Exactly. This may be the hardest thing I'll ever do."

"How can I help?"

"Just pray for me and for all those I will be talking to. But for right now, just listen to me."

So Steffen told the stories of torn and tattered relationships with family and friends across the country: relationships that at one time he "did not give a fart about."

Over the weekend, Steffen wore himself out reconciling himself with others and with his God. His mother told me that Steffen and his father "spent two hours Friday night in his room laughing and crying." He called relatives and friends, spending hours on the phone. With only one exception, all of his local friends came to see him.

Early Monday morning, having done what he felt he had to do, Steffen died. He walked straight through a spiritual opening and into the arms of his God.

PEACE WITH GOD

Orley was in his early eighties, blind and nearly deaf, dying from cardiovascular disease. He was also afflicted by the absence of a

family that seemed to be retaliating for his abuse and abandon-
ment of them. Alone in a care center, angry at his lot in life,
upset at the world, and incensed at something called God, he
was a resident the staff preferred to avoid.

Indeed, he was a handful. But Lisa, the hospice nurse, got
along well with Orley. Lisa was writing history with this recal-
citrant patient, who would have nothing to do with any other
hospice staff, especially the chaplain.

One day, however, while visiting another of our patients at
this same care center, I decided to look in on Orley, say hello,
and cut and run. After introducing myself by virtually scream-
ing into his one good ear, I gained permission to place an assisted
hearing device (AHD) over his head, and we began to talk.
Rather, I began to listen.

Anger poured out of this person as if he were the world
reservoir of anger. Placing the AHD onto his head and saying just
a few words into the microphone seemed to stir an otherwise
lethargic human being into full animation. The words "your family"—flowing from my mouth, into the microphone, and through
the tubing into Orley's ears—seemed to act like ignited dynamite.
The dam blew up, and all the anger roiled out into the small room.

According to Orley, his family did "not care a damn" about
him. In fact, the world was a mean and cruel place: "dog-eat-
dog." As he viewed the matter, "Hell can't be any worse than
what we got right here." The anger, frustration, and invectives
continued. All I could do was listen.

I could have avoided this. I could have just gone home. It
was hardly a condition of employment that I look into this resident's room. It had been a good day. Now, it seemed, I had
snatched defeat from the jaws of victory.

Finally, getting ready to take my leave, I risked inquiring whether he would like a prayer. I really knew the answer, and I was glad that Orley was the one with the AHD in his ears, rather than the other way around.

To my surprise, Orley responded, "It's up to you. Don't matter none to me." It was still an angry tone, but it was permission to proceed.

Aware of the limits of tolerance before me, I intoned a brief prayer, alluding to John 14:1–4 ("I go [to] prepare a place for you"). At first there was no manifest reaction. Then, a slight tear appeared at the corner of one eye, a tear that seemed to catalyze a most remarkable statement: "I never had much room for God in my life, so I don't know if he has a room for me or not."

It was then that Orley began to calmly, but painfully, admit his own role in making the world a less-than-happy place. He confessed that his children had good reason to hate him; in fact, he hated himself.

Orley's God was an elusive God. Since the only God he could envision was a punishing God, it was more comforting for him to believe in no God at all. "What do you think?" he asked.

The question startled me. It had not occurred to me that a person this angry could do anything more than vent. But now, out of the blue, came the unmistakable sign of a willingness to listen. We talked about the God of forgiveness, the God of second and third and multiple chances. We prayed again for forgiveness, and another dam burst. As Orley wept, his body shook and shuddered.

Later that evening, Orley asked for the hospice nurse, Lisa, whom he insisted on calling "Stella." When she arrived, he said to her, "He's still here, isn't he?" Not sure what he was talking about, Lisa asked him to explain.

"That man," Orley said, pointing directly at an empty chair that, in his physical blindness, he couldn't see, "has been sitting here all night. He's waiting for me to go with him. I think it's time for us to go."

Orley died within the hour, having made his peace with his God.

"THE STRAIGHT STORY" OF ALVIN STRAIGHT

In David Lynch's film, *The Straight Story,* we learn the real-life story of a simple man from Laurens, Iowa, who is suddenly faced with a common need for reconciliation. Alvin Straight (Richard Farnsworth), in his late seventies and obviously ill, has just learned from his physician that little can be done to restore his health. Alvin returns home knowing that his time is limited. We have no idea how many years or months the doctor has in mind, but it is clear that Alvin knows that his remaining time is short.

That very evening the telephone rings. Rose (Sissy Spacek), Alvin's daughter who has a speech handicap, takes the call. Alvin learns that his estranged brother Lyle (Harry Dean Stanton) has been hospitalized with a debilitating stroke. At first it appears that the news washes right over Alvin. Soon, however, he informs Rose that he needs to go see Lyle. She offers to drive Alvin the two hundred and eighty miles, since he can no longer drive due to failing eyesight. Alvin declines.

"How are you going to get there then?" Rose asks.

"Don't know yet," Alvin replies. "Haven't got that figured out."

But Alvin comes up with a plan. He builds a trailer, stocks it with food and other necessities, hitches it to his lawn tractor, and heads for Wisconsin from his home in north-central Iowa. He encounters a number of problems along the way: mechanical failure, extreme weather, and challenges of the heart. A newer tractor replaces the original one; the newer one is repaired. The stormy weather breaks, and Alvin's journey continues. A personal journey to forgiveness becomes the odyssey of a stranger who enters into various peoples' lives, bringing reconciliation to their worlds.

On the very last leg of Alvin's trip, his lawn tractor appears to breathe its last on the back road that leads to his brother's shack in the hills. A farmer comes along and encourages Alvin to "give it another try." It is a successful try, and the farmer leads Alvin to Lyle's shack.

Alvin hobbles up to Lyle's weather-beaten abode and calls out to his brother. At first there is no response, but then we see movement inside the dwelling. The door opens, and Alvin's frail brother emerges onto the porch. He positions himself carefully with his walker. Little is said. Finally, Lyle looks toward the lawn tractor with the trailer attached. He turns to look at Alvin and then looks back at the makeshift travel trailer. With tears in his eyes he looks at his brother, with whom he once counted the stars at night and shared dreams, this brother with whom he had dashed the stars from the heavens with mutual words of anger, and asks, "You drove that to come see me?"

"Yep."

We do not witness what may have been said between the reconciling brothers after that initial exchange. They were men of few words. Perhaps words had done enough damage. What we do know is that two brothers facing their own deaths sought and found mutual forgiveness for longstanding hurts. Perhaps pure presence healed the pain. But we wonder: How many nights did the aged brothers sit out on Lyle's front porch, looking up to the heavens and realigning their own stars?

Alvin Straight died two years later.

THE SPIRITUAL CONNECTION

May I pass over effortlessly as an envelope to the other world.
May my breaths release themselves from a wailing mouth, carrier pigeons enroute;
though now alone with a table and chair as I have been all my life,
May somewhere common folk matriculate out of the rubber room of a cold forest,
their hair arrayed with pine needles like sea life,
their coats dusted with plastic, doily flakes of snow,
their arms, unborn, undying,
outstretched in unison like a carousel.

TROY DENT, "HIV, MON
AMOUR #XIX"[5]

The process of forgiveness was not an effortless one for Carl, Steffen, Orley, or Alvin. But it seems certain that each of them valued the task as essential to being able to "pass over effortlessly as an envelope to the other world." Forgiving and seeking forgiveness were missions they could not neglect.

Carl was looking forward to being reunited with Helen. Perhaps she would be joined by other deceased loved ones with arms "outstretched in unison like a carousel." We do know that Carl needed to "go around on the carousel" with Freddie before passing over to that other world.

For Orley it is less clear. But it does seem that despite a lifetime of being out of relationship with God, church, and family, at the very end he managed to reconcile with his God. We do not know exactly how that reconciliation may have occurred, but there is reason to believe that a forgiving God sat patiently in the chair waiting for him. Perhaps his God was simply waiting for this anguished soul to serve out his time in the living hell of his earthly life.

For Steffen the process of reconciliation certainly did not come easily. It wore the life out of him. For Alvin the process of reconciliation with his brother involved a strenuous journey that was physical, emotional, and spiritual as well.

We might say that each one of the people presented here met the challenge laid down by St. Paul to the community of Ephesus (and to us all).

All bitterness, fury, anger, shouting, and
reviling must be removed from you,
along with all malice. [And] be
kind to one another, compassionate,
forgiving one another as God has
forgiven you in Christ.

EPHESIANS 4:31–32

There seems to be something innately human and divine in each of us as we approach the end of life. The drive to be in right relationship with those around us and with our God is played out consistently from one deathbed to another. There are exceptions (see "Bart the Abuser," chapter eleven), but the exceptions merely prove the rule. The Orleys of this world suggest that as we move toward that other world it may never be too late to become squared with God.

QUESTIONS FOR REFLECTION AND DISCUSSION

How does it feel to forgive and to be forgiven?

What needs to happen if I am to "pass over effortlessly as an envelope to the other world"?

How may we see the parable of the prodigal son (Luke 15:11–32) in the stories of Carl, Steffen, Orley, and our own lives?

CHAPTER SEVEN

~

hearing language
from beyond ourselves

*W*hile this entire book pleads the case for listening well to what the dying have to say, the present chapter offers perhaps a harder pill to swallow. It is easy to understand how a dying person might see a deceased loved one at the bedside, but seeing relatives from generations back? How can we repeat what we have never heard or recall what we have never known? How can we perform what we have never practiced, speak a language we have never spoken, or sing a song we've never heard? How is it that just when we think we have lost touch with a loved one from the devastation of Alzheimer's disease, a coma, or death itself, suddenly a connection is made?

While an effort is made here to "explain" the phenomena reported throughout this book, it must be recalled that the purpose of this book is not to explain but to report. The hope behind the reporting of these stories is that each story may become an icon. "Stories," claims writer Madeleine L'Engle, "no matter how simple, can be vehicles of truth; can be, in fact, icons. . . . Stories are able to help us to become more whole, to become Named. And Naming is one of the impulses behind all art; to give a name to the cosmos we see despite all the chaos."[1]

To use the phraseology of today's computerized world, it is hoped that whenever we encounter someone who is dying and speaking of a trip to be taken, we will click on the "icon" for chapter five. As in the case of the computer, when we click on an icon, many options and choices are displayed. Many of the icons presented here offer insights to the truth of what the dying are trying to communicate. Indeed, these icons enable us to sort through the chaos that accompanies the tasks associated with caring for someone who is terminally ill. May these stories help us to focus on some simple truths.

"I DON'T KNOW WHO TO STAND WITH!"

"Do you see them out there?" she asks as I enter our bedroom. My wife, Dawn, seems to be in a lighthearted mood; she is sitting up in the hospital bed looking refreshed and alert.

"See who? See what?"

"Those people in the hallway. The hallway is full of them. How could you miss them?"

"Well, you know me; I have the knack of overlooking details," I respond with a smile.

Dawn laughs her distinctive giggle and then asks, "But how can you miss so many people in a narrow hallway? And especially with all the symbols they are carrying?"

"Dawn, your vision is different from mine these days. Why don't you just tell me about them? Who are these people? Why are they here? What symbols are they carrying?"

"They are the Ritual People, Ron." But as Dawn says this, she turns her head looking just beyond my shoulder into the middle of the room. "They are with her," she says, nodding in the direction of her gaze.

Instinctively, I look around but see nothing and no one. "Who is *she?*"

"Geez, Ron. She is the Ritual Planner."

"Okay, what ritual are we planning now?" It was only a few nights ago, in the wee hours of the morning, that Dawn wanted to plan the sacrament of anointing: a rite that our small Christian Life Community came to celebrate with us. I am curious to know what ritual she is planning with this Ritual Planner, the Ritual People, and all of the symbols they apparently are carrying.

"We are planning ritual number seven."

"What is ritual number seven?" I ask but don't really expect much of a response. So often lately, efforts to gain clarity regarding Dawn's sharings wind up in a dead end. A few days earlier, this woman, who now appears to be the Ritual Planner, had told Dawn to "follow the Four Ways." When I asked Dawn what the Four Ways were, she barely acknowledged my question. No answer was forthcoming.

Suddenly, Dawn reaches over to take my hand, looks me squarely in the eyes, and with her face lit up as if a spotlight were shining upon her, excitedly announces, "It's pretty much like Ritual Number Six, but we're skipping that one. Ritual Number Seven is a welcoming, a celebration. It's going to be great, Ron. I can't wait."

The power in Dawn's grip and the intensity of her excitement convince me that something profound is happening here. Somehow it is all beginning to make sense. Last night our friends were here to ritualize Dawn's readiness to leave us. She knows she is dying. We all know she is dying; and she knows we all know it as well. And so the sacrament of anointing stood as a farewell ritual. Now, it makes sense that a welcoming ritual will be planned for the moment she passes from Here to There.

"What are the symbols that these folks are carrying?" I ask, thinking that she will probably inform me of crosses and chalices.

"It amazes me that you cannot see for yourself, Ron. Anyway, they are carrying flags—red, blue, green, and yellow flags. Everybody has them. They took them on the bus today."

"Were you on the bus with those folks and their flags?"

"Oh, yes, Ron. It was wonderful. You know they had all those flags and were waving them and singing to me."

I asked her what the people were singing. She couldn't recall. "But they were beautiful songs, and they were singing them just for me."

I inquired where the bus was now. She wasn't sure. "Just around. It isn't time to go yet, you know."

I wondered who else had been on the bus with her, and she provided me with a passenger list: the Ritual Planner, the Ritual People, the man with the gray mustache (the bus driver), Bill (the deceased husband of a friend of ours), and her deceased parents. It seems that "Henry and Gloria" were also on the bus, but Dawn was unable to identify them. One thing she was very clear about: they were all deceased.

Later, I again walked into our bedroom and found Dawn sitting up in the bed, fully awake and alert. But what I saw stopped me dead in my tracks. She had a bright smile on her face as she signed a pattern repeatedly with her right arm and hand. Over and over again she traced a square pattern in the air, beginning at a point to her left, moving to a point upward, tracing to her right, then to a point downward, and ending with a flourish straight toward the ceiling. The expression on her face and the nodding of her head let me know that she was not alone.

This was a fascinating show. As the signing repeated itself, Dawn looked to her left across the room. As if she were picking up a nonverbal cue from someone I couldn't see, she smiled and nodded in assent, all the while retracing the pattern. I just watched silently, observing something profound yet, for me, coded and indecipherable.

Finally, the signing ceased and Dawn appeared to be watching the Silent Ones leave the room. As her gaze drifted to the door, she acknowledged my presence. "Oh, I didn't know you were here."

"You were pretty preoccupied. What exactly was going on?"

"What do you mean?"

"Well, I mean you were heavily engaged in doing this." I made the sign that I had observed her tracing in the air time after time. "What's the deal?"

"Oh, it's just stuff. I'm really tired. I need to lie down."

That was it. No further discussion. No insights would ever be gleaned from Dawn's consciousness concerning that which appeared to be so meaningful on a subconscious level.

Somewhere in the midst of these events, I gradually became aware—suspicious at least—that what I was witnessing had a great deal to do with Dawn's Native American heritage. While it was widely known that her father's family history was rooted in a Native culture, not much was ever discussed about it. In fact, Dawn would usually become upset whenever I brought it up in a conversation, especially with other people present.

Now that she was dying, some potent connection with her father's Native culture appeared to be unfolding. That connection became startlingly clear when I entered the bedroom one evening two days before her death.

Again, she was sitting up in bed but in a highly agitated state, pulling on the bed rails and looking frantically from one side of the room to the other. "I don't know what to do. I don't know what to do. I don't know what to do." Dawn repeated this litany over and over again, as I stood there wondering and waiting.

"What's happening, Dawn?" I reached out to take her hand, but she pulled away, regripping the bed rail.

"God, Ron, don't you see them?" There was slightly veiled anger and much frustration in her tone.

"See who? Remember, your vision is often a bit different from mine these days. Tell me about them, Dawn."

"There are all these people here," she explained, gesturing with a wide sweep of her hand. Now I know that this room is full of people from her dying life.

"The Reds are over here." Dawn motioned the width and length of the right side of her bed. "They are carrying white flags. And the Whites are over here," motioning now to the left side of the room, "and they are carrying red flags."

She was becoming increasingly agitated. Selfishly, I thought, *Man, this is going to be a long night, and for the third night in a row no sleep for me.* But I took a step or two closer so that I might hold her in my arms.

Suddenly, she reached out to stop me. "God, Ron, be careful! You walked right into him. Just look where you're going."

"Sorry. There really are a lot of them here then. Is that frightening to you?"

"No, it's not frightening. They're all good people. It's just . . ." She stopped in midsentence, and I could see the tears welling in her eyes. Her brow was furrowed in that familiar way that tells me that she is deeply troubled or distressed. I saw her then as I had twenty-three years before when she had struggled with being pregnant again, a time when the dungeon of depression had entrapped her, another time when I had felt helpless to aid her.

"It's just?" I repeated for her.

"It's just . . . ," she said again, faltering. Then, with a forceful outburst, like a thunderclap with the lightning no more than a second away, she screamed, "It's just that I don't know who to stand with!" While her head sagged to her chest, her arms raised into the air and her fingers stretched out as if they intended to grasp onto something falling from the heavens. As her arms came down, she began to sob. I sat on the edge of the bed and held her. She cried out between sobs: "I don't know who to stand with, Ron. I just don't know who to stand with. I don't know what to do."

Letting her cry and keeping my mouth shut seemed to be the best thing to do right then. Besides, I didn't have a clue.

What could I do? What could I say? What was going on here anyway? While all of this was terribly interesting, it was not a lot of fun. I didn't have the answers. I wasn't even clear on the question.

"Do you need to make a choice?" I heard myself ask.

"Well, I'm not sure. I just don't know. I don't know."

"You said they are all good people, Dawnie. I think they'll help you out of this. Besides, you will figure it out. You always do."

"Maybe. Perhaps you're right. But I just don't have the energy to deal with it." With that comment, she drifted off to sleep.

It became clear to me that evening that while Dawn's Native roots may have been minimally important in her life, they were playing a meaningful role in her dying. The mystery of it all unfolded gradually after her death as I engaged in extensive research on Native American cultures.

There are times in our lives when something immensely powerful and important happens, and for the rest of our lives we can recall where we were, what we felt, what we heard, and what we smelled and tasted; everything surrounding the event and our place in it remains welded to our consciousness. Learning of John F. Kennedy's assassination was one of those events for me. Another such event was the moment I picked up Joseph Epes Brown's book, *The Sacred Pipe: Black Elk's Account of the Seven Rites of the Oglala Sioux.*[2] At that moment I knew I was onto something.

I just stood there at the library shelf looking at the book, trying to stare through it. I wanted to absorb its contents immediately. Yet, at the same time, I wanted to prolong this moment and savor each of the pages. I knew I was holding an important key to understanding Dawn's dying experience—the Ritual

People, the Ritual Planner, Rituals six and seven, maybe even the flags.

Whether it is *The Sacred Pipe,* William K. Powers's *Oglala Religion,*[3] or John Neihardt's *Black Elk Speaks,*[4] the seven rites tend to be discussed in the same order. While not referred to by number, such as "ritual number seven," the sixth one mentioned is the Girl's Puberty Ritual. For a woman fifty-one years old, it is no wonder that they skipped this particular rite.

Ritual number seven corresponds to the Throwing of the Ball *(Tapa Wankayeyapi)* ceremony, where the ball represents *Wankantanka,* the Great Spirit and "symbolic knowledge." There are teams involved in this ritual, and they represent "people scrambling to be close to the spirits" as well as "the struggle of people submerged in ignorance to free themselves."[5]

It is ritual number five, however, that intrigued me the most. The Making of a Relative (*Hunkalowanpi* or *Hunkapi)* is the ritualizing of a friendship bond that goes beyond that of kinship.[6] As I consulted the sources concerning the meaning and characteristics of these rites, I remembered the obvious and important friendship that had emerged on the bus between Dawn and the others she encountered there. But when I learned that this same ritual is normally done with flags, my interest was ratcheted up at least one more notch. According to William K. Powers, in the *Hunkalowanpi* rite, "Wands (*huinkata-cannunpa,* literally, Hunka 'pipes') are waved over the participants (*hunkakazopi* or 'wand' waving)."[7]

William Stolzman, in his book *The Pipe and Christ: A Christian-Sioux Dialogue,* notes that "The Lakota surround themselves with flags of different colors, reminding them of the major spirits of the Pipe."[8] He observes that with regard to yet another of the seven Sioux rites, the Sun Dance, cans are placed at each corner of the *Yuwipi* (Sun Dance) altar where *Wanunyanpt* (offerings) are placed. "Colored cloths are attached to slim willow canes *(Sagye)*. The colors represent the Four Directions with most often the directional color symbolism expressed by black for the West, red for the North, yellow for the East, and white for the South."[9]

My research caused me to take careful note of William K. Powers's further observation that "in contemplative or verbal prayer, offerings are made to the four directions, the zenith and nadir, and the universe."[10] I recalled that the evening when Dawn was signing and doing so repeatedly with those visible only to herself, she had referred to the "Four Ways."

Finally, the *Hunkalowanpi* or *Hunka* ritual is also known as the *Lowanpi* (i.e., "they sing") or the *alowanpi* (i.e., "they sing on or over"). How important it was to Dawn that those on the bus, those Ritual People, had sung to her. According to Stolzman, "the medicine men consider it crucial to have songs at the *Lowanpi* because their spirits will not come or give answers or go and do what they are supposed to do unless songs are sung."[11]

Friendship and flags, singing and signing—and all of this from a woman who consciously knew so little of her Native background!

Examples abound where the unfamiliar culture of the dying's ancestors has defined their final moments of life. Jack, a seventy-eight-year-old man with end-stage Alzheimer's disease, suddenly began singing in German, the language of his grandparents. According to Jack's family, he had never spoken German in his life, let alone sung it.

Greg, a thirty-four-year-old man dying of cancer, exhibited similar behavior. According to his parents, who were caring for him, on the day of his death, he suddenly began speaking "gibberish." They naturally assumed that it was the "morphine speaking." Late that morning, Greg's grandmother walked into his room as the "morphine" was speaking. She immediately recognized what was transpiring. He was speaking in Danish, a language he had never known, and a language he had never spoken or read. In Danish, Greg asked his grandmother to tell everyone he loved them. His final gift to his family was wrapped up and tied together with the roots of his ancestral tongue.

My guess is that far more instances of latent cultures emerging at the time of death occur than we know of or can imagine. We do not know about them because we convince ourselves that the morphine is speaking and refuse to really listen. Furthermore, the necessary interpreters or translators may not be present.

"THE GAME IS OVER"

Liz is an eighty-eight year old suffering the silent but ruthless ravages of Alzheimer's disease. It has been a long time since she has been able to connect with reality. She can have conversations; they just don' make a lot of sense. Luther, her faithful ninety-year-old husband, walks the two blocks to the nursing home three times a day to bring her flowers from the garden of their in-town home.

I have been visiting Liz and Luther for nearly a year now. I know what to expect. Whether he is there or not, Liz will be in her bed, and when I walk into her room she will glance toward the window and say, "That's a good ball game out there," referring to a small plot of grass with a crab apple tree in the middle and not a lot of room for a ball game. However, Liz seems to enjoy watching "them" play.

If Luther is there with her, she will be asking him, "Did you get the chores done? How are the cows doing? Did you get them milked? Now don't forget to feed the pigs. Bring me the eggs; I'll package them up." While they still own the farm outside of town, Luther has not farmed the land for nearly thirty years. He is renting the farm. They gave up raising hogs forty years ago. Liz has not candled an egg for nearly fifty years. But that's the way it is with Alzheimer's: the past is far more present than the present.

The door is open, but as I reach in to knock I notice an unusual scene. Liz is sitting in a wheelchair. In all this time I have never seen her out of bed. Luther is sitting on the edge of a comfortable overstuffed chair. His head is bowed. They are holding hands.

For a moment I am reconsidering whether I should break the spell of this couple enjoying each other's company. But just as I am about to turn on my heels and leave, Luther looks up, smiles, and greets me with his everwelcoming "Good to see you." It is then that I notice that the cheery greeting betrays the tears glistening on his cheeks.

"I really do not wish to disturb you two. I can come back another time."

"No, no. You're not disturbing us. We were just sitting here."

"Now, Luther, it seems to me you were doing something more than just sitting here. I see tears. Want to tell me what's really going on? You certainly don't have to tell me. But I promise to listen, if it will help."

Liz, who is wearing her favorite sweatshirt with a pair of kittens embossed on the front, looks up at me without her trademark smile. "No one's playing ball. The ball game's over." Liz appears troubled with a sadness I have never before seen.

"The ball game's over—that's for sure," Luther affirms. I smile at his comment, thinking that Luther is playing along with Liz, but I quickly take note that he is not smiling. He is dead serious.

"The ball game is over?" I repeat.

"We are going to lose the farm," Luther says, the agony in his voice reflecting deep despair.

As Luther is crying, Liz reaches over to take his hand. She pulls him forward and gently draws her grieving husband into her arms. Luther is sobbing now; Liz is crying softly. I stand amazed at the scene unfolding in front of me.

"Why?" Liz asks.

Luther looks up at his wife of nearly seventy years and explains, "In order to care for you here."

"Why didn't you tell me?" Liz asks.

Startled and confused, Luther looks at me and then turns to Liz. "Because . . . because . . . well, I figured you wouldn't remember anyway."

And Liz, with the assurance that comes from having raised a family of six, coordinated untold numbers of community and church events, handled the finances of home and farm—this woman who has been unable to connect with the world around her for years now—tells the man of her life and love, "I know. But I need to know."

Liz had no knowledge of this interchange the next day. The destructive dynamics of Alzheimer's resumed within seconds of that one clear moment her husband will never forget.

Just as Dawn, Greg, and Jack connected in their dying days and hours with a culture consciously unknown to them, Liz re-connected with the world around her and her troubled husband at a time when no one thought it was possible. We must never stop listening to the dying.

Liz died two weeks after this event. There was never another moment when Luther would have any real sense that Liz knew he was even there. There was never another ball game outside her window. The ball game was truly over. Luther knew to his dying day that for a moment in time, Liz knew what was going on, and for that same brief moment he had his precious partner back to have and to hold, and to be held by.

"I LOVE YOU, SON"

On January 15, 1939, I was born at home on my family's farmstead in central New York State. My mother was twenty-six years old; my father would be forty in just six short weeks. Mom and Dad had already been married for nine years. They had survived the Great Depression; later they would survive the Depression-like years of World War II. Eventually, they would even survive having two sons.

In truth, there were many moments when I doubted I would survive the sometimes verbally violent barrages from my father and his intrusive forays into my affairs. Dad's vitriolic attack when I showed up at home one day with a

"Kennedy for President" bumper sticker on my car was topped only by his threat to ban me from the farmstead when he learned from a friend that I'd registered as a Democrat. In a rock-ribbed Republican town, this was like having a turncoat for a son.

I should have seen it coming that day when Dad ranted and raved about my relationship with Dawn, something he could know only from reading her letters sent to me from college during the four years of our dating. A few years after this particular blowup, which generated some of my most acidic remarks, I announced to my parents that Dawn and I were getting married. Dad informed me then that since Dawn's father was "Indian," my children would be "Red Indians" and "they will be no grandchildren of mine."

This father–son relationship enabled me to learn the techniques of confrontation as well as passive resistance in dealing with conflict.

Though I had written Mom and Dad a "love letter" about two years before Dad's death, I never once heard my dad tell me he loved me. Dad's only response to my letter was: "I burned that damned letter. I don't need your love." While I knew he probably loved me in his own way, I longed to hear him say it. When Dad died of a sudden heart attack in November 1974, the possibility of the words "I love you, Son" died with him in the ambulance—or so I thought.

During the summer of 1985, while studying at Regis University in Denver, Colorado, I decided to become familiar with Ira Progoff's journaling methodology.[12] After reading and outlining his book, *At a Journal Workshop,* I began the process.

1. The *Daily Log:* an inventory of feelings, thoughts, impressions; a rendering of self in the midst of daily events and encounters.
2. The *Period Log:* an assessment of where I was with life at that particular time, including job, family, health, feelings, and awareness of my surroundings.
3. The development of an extensive *Life History Log* from birth to the present moment. It was here that I first encountered the issue of my relationship with my father, but it was a "hit-and-run" consideration of our contentious relationship.
4. The delineation of *Stepping Stones,* significant events, movements, and moments in the unfolding of my life. The father–son relationship was ignored.
5. A listing of *Present Relationships, Past Relationships, and Persons Not Now Living.* Dad was at the top of the latter list.
6. After reviewing all of the twenty-eight names on the three lists, I placed an asterisk next to "Dad," knowing that it was with my father that I would begin an intensive journal process.

It was a beautiful Saturday in July. When my feet hit the floor, I knew it was going to be the day when I would engage in a *Dialogue with Persons,* certainly with Dad, and most likely with one or two others. Initially, I just sat with pen and notebook, eyes closed, moving into a *Twilight State* where I was neither asleep nor fully awake, just resting with the *Now Moment.* The only sounds were the birds chirping outside my window, an occasional door shutting, and a few footsteps.

Soon, my pen began moving, writing a narrative account of my relationship with Dad. Much of what was written in the narrative is outlined below, with the addition of short accounts of the three moments when Dad and I had really talked, the best moments I ever had with Dad.

Next, I concentrated on the *Stepping Stones* in my father's life. I listed forty-seven of these events in the first person, as if Dad were developing the list himself. Some of the events follow.

1. I was born February 27, 1899.
2. I moved to the farm with Mom and Dad around 1905.
3. I dropped out of school at the end of ninth grade in 1913: mixed emotions; I liked school.
4. I decided not to return to business school in Syracuse in 1915: disappointed, but was needed at home.
6. Offered an opportunity in 1920 to go to South America with a Syracuse businessman; turned it down because my mother had a fit. I was really disappointed.
7. Took over the farm in 1921.
8. Met your mom at Lulu's Tea Kitchen (1929); I was so excited.
10. My father died, 1936: a sad day.
12. You were born, 1939: I felt so relieved.
20. You graduated from high school, 1957: I felt so proud.
21. You announced your engagement to Dawn, 1960: I was angry.
22. You graduated from college, 1961: I felt pretty neutral about it.

45. We sold the farm, 1972: I felt distressed.

46. My heart attack, 1973: I was afraid.

47. The brush fire, November 20, 1974: I felt frightened, humiliated, but finally freed of it all.

Returning to a *Twilight State* and just sitting with this list of *Stepping Stones* in my head, I soon became vaguely aware that my pen was moving down the page. Some of the dialogue with my deceased father is noted below with *R* for me and *D* for my father.

R: Hi, Dad. It has been a long time since I've seen you.

D: Yes, it has. How are you?

R: Real fine, thanks. Have you been able to keep up with us?

D: No—it seems like we have really been out of touch.

R: Yes, I know. In fact, I think we have always been out of touch.

D: We did have a problem communicating, I guess.

R: Well, it certainly wasn't all your fault.

D: Maybe so. But I guess I never really could understand you. You seemed to have interests that I couldn't understand. Besides, you were too much like me.

R: You mean we are both kind of bullheaded?

D: Yeah, that's it. But I saw you as having more drive to make it in the world than I ever had.

R: Did you kind of wish you had gotten away from the farm as I did?

D: You bet! You know, I regretted giving in to my mother and always felt trapped.

R: So you felt cheated?

D: Yes, and I guess I felt envious of you.

The dialogue went on in this vein—an opening up to each other. And then:

R: There seems to have been some undefinable thing between us.
D: Is it that you never knew if I loved you?
R: I think that is it, Dad.
D: Well, Son, I want you to know that I do love you and have always loved you. I just didn't know how to show it. Forgive me. Can you forgive me, Ronald? I do love you very much!
R: Thanks, Dad. Yes, I forgive you. But you must forgive me too. I was bullheaded, totally insensitive to you and Mom. There you were, fifty-eight years old when I was a senior in high school, trying to understand a generation so different from your own. And I'd stay out late at night, never telling you and Mom when I would be back. You were probably worried that I would get in a wreck or get Dawn pregnant. I would tell you all this great wisdom I was getting in college—and, I think I purposely challenged some of your ideas just to get a reaction from you. In fact, knowing that you were a strong Republican and not a fan of Catholics had something to do with my decision to become both a Democrat and a Catholic. I was an adolescent in rebellion.
D: Yes, all of those things were troubling. I just didn't know how to talk to you about them.
R: As I look back, I am really amazed at how you kept your cool as much as you did.
D: What do you mean?

R: Well, despite my late nights out, you never laid down any law.

D: I was afraid you would leave home.

R: You mean you really wanted me to stay?

D: I love you, my son!

The above is but a small portion of the dialogue I had with my father that morning, eleven years after his death. Dad never made it west of the Ohio River during his seventy-five years of life. That morning, he was very much present to me and with me in Denver, Colorado. When I finally looked up at the clock, nearly three hours had passed, and I had written nearly a dozen pages—the longest, most in-depth conversation with my father ever.

After silently reading our dialogue, I felt slightly teary, regretful, and a strange sensation of Dad's real presence. A feeling of longing came over me. "Don't go, Dad. Stay here, please."

Dad honored my plea. As I began reading the dialogue aloud, my father's presence could not have been stronger. A strange tingling feeling began in my legs, similar to the chill one experiences when imagining an eerie presence late at night. But this was a most welcome presence. The tingling began the journey up to my thighs. Then it lessened. As Dad and I came to the end of our discussion, the tingling resumed and ran all the way up my body, from my thighs to my torso and my arms, to my shoulders and my neck, and then to my eyes, where the tingling turned to tears.

"Tell your Mom that I love her too," he said. "And, Son, I think we got a good crop coming up." The tears came rushing, pouring forth. I was overwhelmed with gratitude for finally having a functional and loving relationship with my father. The only other time I cried with such intensity was seven years later, when I said good-bye to Dawn as she died.

THE SPIRITUAL CONNECTION

Jesus took Peter, James, and John and led them up a high mountain apart by themselves. And he was transfigured before them. . . . Then Elijah appeared to them along with Moses, and they were conversing with Jesus. Then Peter said to Jesus in reply, "Rabbi, it is good that we are here! . . ." He hardly knew what to say, they were so terrified. Then a cloud came, casting a shadow over them; then from the cloud came a voice, "This is my beloved Son. Listen to him." Suddenly, looking around, they no longer saw anyone but Jesus alone with them. As they were coming down from the mountain, [Jesus] charged them not to relate what they had seen to anyone, except when the Son of Man had risen from the dead. So they kept the matter to themselves, questioning what rising from the dead meant.

MARK 9:2, 4–5A, 6–8, 9–10

Peter, James, and John certainly were not dying, but they did have the strange experience of seeing, for a brief moment, Elijah and Moses return from the dead. It was a moment of transfiguration for Jesus and a transforming event for the three disciples. Peter, James, and John would never be the same.

Peter, James, and John—like Dawn, who *was* in the active dying process—heard a language beyond themselves. Indeed, they each witnessed a rising from the dead. Dawn never seemed to have questioned what or whom she saw. Neither, apparently, did any of the many others noted throughout this book who witnessed some event of the dead arising in their very presence.

Nowhere in the four scriptural references to this same transfiguration event do the disciples appear to question what they saw.[13] All they ever seem to question is what Jesus means when he talks of the Son of Man rising from the dead.

We have come to understand, however, that what Peter, James, and John witnessed was a dramatic highlighting of the "purpose of both the law and the prophets . . . to prepare for Christ."[14] To prepare for one's God also appears to be a purpose for all of the events recounted within this book.

As I found forgiveness in the dialogue with my father many years after his death, so too did I experience a sense of a forgiving God's real presence. As Luther heard Liz speak a language way beyond what he ever thought possible for her to regain, perhaps he learned more than to not give up on listening to the dying; perhaps he learned as well that our God does not give up on us.

As we observe how Dawn, Greg, and Jack connected with the latent cultures of their ancestral heritages, we are left with the wonderment and mystery of a God who is the God for all time, the God for all peoples. We are reminded all over again that this God can show up in the unlikeliest of places: on a mountaintop, in the midst of one's ancestors mysteriously present in one's bedroom, or in the sudden coherence of a victim of Alzheimer's disease.

QUESTIONS FOR REFLECTION AND DISCUSSION

How have I experienced the love of God in the death of a loved one?

How are my ancestors present still in my family's life?

What have been my mountaintop experiences?

CHAPTER EIGHT

near-life experiences:

the conversation stopper

*I*t is one thing for the dying to experience the presence of deceased friends and relatives as they inch closer to that mystical and sacred time when the reunion beyond this life occurs. It is understood that the dying might even express themselves in the context of a culture unknown to them but undeniably rooted in their ancestors. We can accept how it is that even an Alzheimer's patient can have a fleeting moment of pre-Alzheimer's normality. And we can make room intellectually for the possibility that in some inexplicable way we can connect with the spirit of a deceased loved one by intently and intentionally focusing on that person.

But dare we believe that it is possible to actually see, hear, feel, and smell people who have already died? Well, that is a bit much. This sort of talk smacks of ghost stories around the campfire.

Yet, these sorts of contact with the dead are what we have come to call near-life experiences (NLE). These experiences are similar to the near-death experience and nearing death awareness in that all three are encounters with the deceased. What is different is that those who have an NLE are not in the process of dying but tend to be perfectly healthy in mind, body, and spirit. The problem is that those having an NLE often do not understand what is happening, and neither do those with whom they choose to share the experience. Typically, the one who has had the NLE entertains the thought that he or she is imagining things, and when a person dares to reveal the experience, the reaction of others, whether verbal or nonverbal, is "You're crazy!"

Perhaps the stories that follow are not as dramatic or improbable as those presented in the movie *Field of Dreams*,[1] in which Ray Kinsella (Kevin Costner) actually sees and interacts with a whole baseball team of deceased players, including "Shoeless Joe" Jackson (Ray Liotta). Certainly, the stories related here are not on the scale of the movie *Ghost*,[2] in which Patrick Swayze plays the ghost of a man invisibly returning to protect his wife from the man who killed him. Instead, these stories are more on the scale of *Sleepless in Seattle*,[3] in which, for a brief moment, Sam Baldwin (Tom Hanks) sees his deceased wife. Most of these experiences are subtle but very distinctive to the people who have them.

A FATHER–DAUGHTER BOND

Not long ago, the mother of a thirteen-year-old girl asked if I would visit her daughter Elissa, who was troubled by recurring visions of her father, who had died six weeks before. Melissa, the mother, was concerned not so much by Elissa's visions or even the frequency of them. Her chief concern was Elissa's anxiety in response to the visionary episodes. Elissa was even seeing her father at school. An otherwise bright and productive student was pleading more and more to be excused from school due to apparent anxiety attacks.

Elissa talked freely about the relationship she had enjoyed with her father. Until the cancer confined him to the house, she and her dad would often go fishing together. One of her fondest memories was how the two of them would sit under the stars at night, sharing their visions of the star formations, imagining life on distant planets, and wondering if others were looking back at them from universes unknown.

Elissa's first vision of her father had occurred only about ten days before I met with her. She was in the cafeteria line at school. As she picked up her tray, she looked down the line, and off to the side stood her father, smiling at her. He seemed to be saying something to her but she could not hear him. She began to walk toward him, and he disappeared. He appeared to her, not as the dad who was wasted away by cancer, but as the dad she had known a few years before, a man who was strong and healthy, full of life and love.

Elissa denied being frightened by the vision or afraid of her dad. "It's just weird." He had by this time appeared to her three times at school and once, the previous Sunday morning, at the foot of her bed. He was always smiling. He was always speaking to her, but she could not hear him. Elissa found some comfort in these visions. "I kept saying after he died how I wished I could see him one more time." Then Elissa summed it all up once again: "But it's so weird. Do you think I'm crazy?"

"No, I sure don't, Elissa. Do you?"

"Well, I don't think so, but this isn't normal. I just wish I knew why. Like, what is he trying to tell me?"

"What do you think he's trying to say to you?"

Elissa sat with that question for what felt like a long, long time. I wondered, as I sat in the silence with her, if I had asked too many teacherlike questions. Had I come to a dead end with this bereaved daughter who was at a dead end herself?

Finally, Elissa responded. "I think he's trying to tell me that everything is going to be okay; that Mom will be fine; that we will be able to stay right here without moving; and that I will be okay. It's strange, you know. My boyfriend and I had broken up that morning, and I was so upset."

"What morning?"

"The morning I first saw Dad in the cafeteria. I think he knew how upset I was, and he was just trying to comfort me, that's all. But it's so weird."

"Elissa, I think you have it figured out. Obviously, you and your dad had a very special relationship. You know, we say that death is not the end of a relationship. It is very common for people to experience a sense of the presence of a deceased loved one. It is less common for the one left behind to actually see the deceased, but it does happen. As a matter of fact, my mother-in-law saw her mother fifteen years after the death. It happened on a Sunday. My mother-in-law said, 'I bet she came back to wind the clock. She always wound the clock on Sundays.' And guess what—when we checked the grandfather clock, which had not run for fourteen years, we discovered that it was fully wound and running. It's 'weird,' as you say.

"Since your mother told me about these experiences you were having, I brought this along to share with you. The poet John Milton wrote it three hundred and fifty years ago. He wrote this sometime after his wife had died."

Methought I saw my late espoused Saint
Brought to me like Alcestis from the grave,
Whom Jove's great Son to her glad Husband gave,
Rescu'd from death by force though pale and faint.
Mine as whom washt from spot of child-bed taint,
Purification in the old Law did save,
And such, as yet once more I trust to have
Full sight of her in Heaven without restraint,
Came vested all in white, pure as her mind:
Her face was vail'd, yet to my fancied sight,
Love, sweetness, goodness, in her person shin'd
So clear, as in no face with more delight.
But O as to embrace me she enclin'd
I wak'd, she fled, and day brought back my night.

JOHN MILTON, "ON HIS
DECEASED WIFE"[4]

After I finished reading, Elissa sat quietly. Finally, she asked, "So, he really saw her? Like I have seen my dad?"

"Well, it is a little different than in your case. He didn't see his deceased wife in a school cafeteria, and the fact is that he had never seen her before in all his life. Milton was blind when he met her. So he never really saw her. That is what he means by the last line: 'I wak'd, she fled, and day brought back my night.'"

"Wow. Then I'm not crazy, after all."

A few days later, Melissa informed me that Elissa's teacher had called, wondering what had happened: "The old Elissa has returned." She had changed from the withdrawn and anxious person the teachers did not recognize to the carefree but focused student they knew as the real Elissa. All that Elissa needed was someone to listen to her and affirm the reality of her experience.

SHADOWS AND PERFUME, CANNONBALLS AND DOVES

The morning I stopped by to see how he was doing after the death of his wife, Gordon could hardly contain himself. He needed to share an experience he did not fully understand. Midge had died nearly six weeks before. It had been a long drawn-out ordeal. Gordon had insisted on caring for her at home until the constant work took its toll on his health. In the final two weeks of Midge's life, Gordon had reluctantly consented to placing his wife of fifty-five years in the local nursing center.

He had weathered the role of primary caregiver, the transfer of his beloved to the last place where either one of them ever wanted to be, her death as he sat at her side, the funeral, and the empty house. But this morning something strange had happened, something completely outside of any experience his seventy-seven years had shown him.

"I'm so glad you're here. You'll understand what happened here this morning. I got up as usual, at 6:30, and went out to the kitchen to get the coffee going. Come with me for a minute out to the kitchen. I want to show you something."

As we stood in the kitchen, Gordon handed me a cup of coffee and said, "Look right through there. As you know, that room was our bedroom. As I stood here this morning with a cup in my hand, I saw her. Well, I mean, I didn't really see her, but I saw a shadow pass by the door. Then I saw the shadow move toward the bed and back by the door. Thought I would go check it out. So I walked a beeline from here to the door-way. Again, I saw the shadow move toward that window you can see from right here. But it wasn't just a shadow; I know it was Midge's shadow. I also smelled her perfume. How can that be when our daughters took all of her cosmetics with them more than a month ago? How does one make sense of it?"

"How do you make sense of it?" I asked.

"Well, I just know it was her perfume, and I'm convinced it was her shadow. So maybe I've gone off the deep end. Maybe I'm crazy."

As I talked with Gordon, it was clear that he wasn't frightened by the experience. Indeed, he claimed it was a most reassuring event for him. He had a sense that Midge was still looking out for him, even from beyond the grave. Eventually, I shared the essence of another man's experience of "seeing" his deceased wife. While I did not have John Milton's poem with me, Gordon agreed that it was easier to understand his own expe-rience in "seeing" Midge than Milton's in seeing his deceased wife, especially since Milton was blind and never did see his wife while she was alive.

In some reported cases, people encounter phenomena that they know beyond any doubt is a sign of a deceased person's presence. In many instances, the encounter serves to announce the news of that person's death. My great-aunt Elizabeth, who was ninety when she died in 1951, told of how she learned that her older brother had been killed in the Civil War. She awoke one night to see a "hot fiery ball, like a cannonball," circle her house three times. "I knew then that Thad was dead. A few days later, three soldiers arrived at our farm, one of them an officer, to inform us that Thad had been killed by a cannonball."

St. Benedict had a similar experience. Benedict's sister, Scholastica, ultimately followed her brother to Monte Cassino to join the Benedictine order. It was their custom as brother and sister to leave their respective monastic communities once a year to spend a day together. One such day in or about the year 547, these two siblings "spent the whole day praising God and talking of sacred things. As night fell they had supper together." But as the evening progressed and the day was drawing to a close, Scholastica said to Benedict, "Please do not leave me tonight." Benedict reminded his sister that he could not possibly remain outside any longer.

As St. Gregory the Great tells the story,[5] Scholastica prayed to God, the skies opened up, lightning flashed, thunder roared, and no one was able to move. Finally, Benedict said to his sister: "May God forgive you, sister. What have you done?"

"Well," she answered, "I asked you and you would not listen, so I asked my God and he did listen. So now go off, if you can, leave me and return to your monastery."

Scholastica was, you might say, more than a little annoyed with her brother. She also demonstrated that she knew how to get her way: "Reluctant as he was to stay of his own will, he remained against his will."

St. Gregory recounts that only three days later, as Benedict was looking up at the sky, "he saw his sister's soul leave her body in the form of a dove, and fly up to the secret places of heaven."

THE CONVERGENCE OF NDE, NDA, AND NLE

Darin was a forty-nine-year-old Vietnam War veteran dying of massive cancer invasion, most likely caused by Agent Orange. "My name should be on the Vietnam wall in D.C.," he once said. "I'm just a late casualty, that's all." He told his wife, Karen, and his mother, Diane, that he'd seen his deceased grandmother at his bedside and that he found comfort in seeing his buddies Joey, Stevie, Anderson, and Merwald, all from "516" (perhaps his unit), all casualties in Vietnam. In addition, Darin mentioned seeing Jesus. "They are waiting for me."

"Is that frightening to you?" I asked Karen as we sat at the dining-room table while her husband slept. His mother was sitting across from me next to Karen.

"No. I've been there. You see I had an NDE years ago when I was fifteen. I went through this tunnel. A warm light kept getting stronger and stronger, brighter and brighter, more and more comforting. I saw this beautiful garden. I just wanted to stay right there." Karen, who was in her middle forties but looked deceptively younger, maintained her composure as she related her story.

"Then why did you come back?" I asked.

"Because Jesus told me I had work to do. I pleaded with him to let me stay, but he kept telling me to go back; and he gradually disappeared. I woke up, finally, in a hospital room. It was shortly after Darin and I started dating. I always thought he was what Jesus meant. Jesus knew I had a life to live with Darin and a family to raise with him. So you see, when my husband says he has seen Jesus, I know exactly what that means."

Darin's mother had been listening intently to her daughter-in-law's story. This mother, who had yet to allow herself to cry over the fate of her son (a reluctant draftee being devoured by a very eager cancer), began to speak in the midst of a flood of tears. "The same . . ." she began, but was overwhelmed with emotion. Karen reached over and took her mother-in-law in her arms. "The same thing happened to me," Diane finally blurted out.

We let Diane take the time and space she needed to release the store of tears and pain that held not only her dying son but also an apparent unresolved issue from her past. Is this why Diane had been unable to cry? Is this why she had seemed unable to accept her son's prognosis?

Finally, she told the story of how things went bad during a surgery she had had when she was thirty-five years old. She too saw a beautiful garden, a tunnel, and a warm bright light. She too saw Jesus, who was beckoning to her, but she did not want to go. "I pleaded and pleaded with him to let me go back. At first he refused. I screamed at him, 'No, you must let me return to my children. You can't leave them without a mother like I was left without my mother.'"

After another long interlude of tears, she went on to explain that her mother had died on an operating table when Diane was very young. "Karen, I never heard you tell about your experience before, but then I never told anyone about mine either, not even my husband. I heard Darin talk about seeing Jesus, but it wasn't until you told of your NDE that I recalled my own. You know, I don't want my son to die, but I think I can let him go now. I will miss him, but I have a pretty good idea what lies ahead for him. I just didn't want to go there when I had the chance. Darin is ready to go. His buddies, my mom, Jesus are all waiting for him."

THE SPIRITUAL CONNECTION

Then afterward I will pour out
my spirit upon all mankind.
Your sons and daughters shall prophesy,
your old men shall dream dreams,
your young men shall see visions;
Even upon the servants and the handmaids,
in those days, I will pour out my spirit.

JOEL 3:1–2

The prophet Joel seemed to understand that, in the perfect world to come, old men would experience images, ideas, and emotions while they slept. He envisioned (because, as a prophet, he learned through visions) young men undergoing mystical experiences and glimpsing various dimensions of the world beyond themselves.

As noted elsewhere in this book, the visions experienced by the dying are claimed and understood to be more than dreams. To the extent that most who die are old men and old women, the experience of the dying puts the lie to Joel's notion that the

old "shall dream dreams." Rather, the dying—young and old—
see visions. If we take to heart the meaning of the Sanskrit
derivative *veda,* we learn that a vision is "to have seen, to know."[6]

For the bereaved the phenomenon is less certain, perhaps because *they* are less certain. Most grieving people who
encounter visions of the deceased know beyond any doubt that
they are not merely dreaming. They simply are not accustomed
to having such experiences. Also, they are acutely aware of how
others will react to the telling of the story.

The bereaved are ready with their defenses: "Maybe I'm
crazy!" The dying are defenseless; they simply tell it like it is.

A new way of knowing occurs for both the dying and the
bereaved who experience visions. As Evelyn Underhill describes
it, "There is a certain duality in our life." In other words, there
are two ways of knowing: the "intuitive" way and the "logical"
way. The intuitive way "knows by communion, not by observation. It cannot give a neat account of its experience . . . [This]
kind of knowledge is more like bathing in a fathomless ocean,
or breathing an intangible and limitless air. It gives contact and
certitude, but not understanding."[7]

Indeed, the visions encountered by either the dying or the
bereaved bring a certain certitude but in no way the kind of
understanding that one needs to explain the occurrence. But is
explanation essential? In the end, all that is essential may be the
understanding of how the visions of the dying and the visions
of the bereaved are sacramental signs of God at work in our lives.[8]

QUESTIONS FOR REFLECTION AND DISCUSSION

What have been the most powerful dreams that I have ever experienced?

What are the stories from my family lore that relate to dreams and visions?

How are these dreams and visions sacramental signs of God at work in my life and/or in the life of my family?

~>

CHAPTER NINE

tuning in to explanations

$\mathcal{M}$arian sees her deceased husband pacing, waiting for her. Granny's deceased son is building her a shed where she can store her things. Mick's dying father tells him to "keep hammering on the wall." Margaret sees "them" coming for her, and she is frightened. Sheila begs her deceased infant to "come to Momma." Callie sees Charles coming closer and closer to her day by day. Mahler sees the "strange lady"; Chopin sees his mother. Burt wants his airline tickets; Clint hears the "train coming"; Duncan sees the horses in the window; Dawn gets a ticket for the bus. Ruth Anne Dodge sees the angel in the prow of a boat and hears the beckoning call. Carl needs to ride the carousel with Freddie. Dawn doesn't know "who to stand with," but she seems to know the rituals of the Oglala without being aware of them. A son is able to reconcile with his deceased father through the medium of writing as if the page *were* his father. Milton the blind poet sees his "late espoused Saint" whom he had never seen. Gordon sees Midge's shadow and smells her perfume. Elissa sees her deceased father at school and at the foot of her bed. All of these and more, plus the tens of thousands of similar stories that are out there in the world, in every nation and culture, beg the question: How can this be?

THE SPIRITUAL JOURNEY FROM HERE TO THERE

How do we explain these odd experiences of NDE, NDA, and NLE? Much of any credible understanding comes through the lens of Jungian theory. According to psychoanalyst Carl Jung, life is a process whereby each of us engages in the building of "the wholeness of [our own] personality . . . a task of the whole life . . . a preparation for death." From this view we are to understand that all of life, whether we realize it or not, is a process of preparing for the end. Jung makes the further claim that as we grow older, "the more veiled becomes the outside world, steadily losing in colour, tone, and passion, the more urgently the inner world calls us."[1]

For the dying, the outside world becomes less and less important or relevant. The process of withdrawal overtakes what was once a near-total outward orientation to life. The orientation now focuses on death and what is perceived to be the circumstance to follow. This withdrawing from the life of the living occurs whether the person dying is five or a hundred and five years of age.

As the movement toward the inner world continues, it is not difficult to understand how the individual may journey away from the labored world of the ego, which Jung identifies with the conscious realm of our psyche, our experience of the empirical world around us. The dying person journeys away from the physical world and toward one much less familiar. This world toward which the dying travel is the deeply inner world; Jung called it the "personal unconscious." [2]

As we live in various states of good health, we are never directly and cognitively in touch with our personal unconscious, the "forgotten or repressed material," the stuff we have lost hold of mentally, or the stuff we have intentionally packed away to avoid remembering. Such a connection requires the assistance of a counselor, a psychiatrist, or a psychotherapist who can help us recall the forgotten or repressed material. The dying, however, move uncontrollably to a "state of diminished consciousness." [3] This diminished consciousness enables the dying to travel back and forth between a state of normal alertness, orientation, and selfhood to a realm of reality previously unknown to them. The diminished consciousness state allows the individual to remember the forgotten, release the repressed, and tune in to the world of the "collective unconscious."

However, before we move to the collective unconscious, let us take up the issue of how Milton could see his "late espoused Saint," how I could experience a sense of my father's presence, how Gordon could smell his wife's perfume, how Elissa could see her dad. At the risk of oversimplifying, the near-life experience happens in the same way as a nearing-death awareness. The only difference is that while the dying may not return, those granted a near-life experience do not leave. The similarity between the two is that both, at least for a moment, enter the realm of the "twilight" world.[4] It is while in the twilight state that we are able to intuit the "flow of our life" and to observe "the other-than-conscious side" of our lives.[5]

Whatever the case, whether it is Darin seeing Jesus, Dawn communicating with the Ritual People, Elissa communicating with her deceased father, Annie "flying with the animals," or my dad and I "talking out" our relationship via my journal, the experiences are all the same. They are the same in that what has been encountered is a sense of relationship to the "interior workings of life," a "sense of participation in the movements of the cosmos" that always comes with "a great intensity" and "great emotional affect." There is always an "awareness of a special light—a luminosity carrying a sense of transcendent validity, authenticity, and essential divinity."[6]

The person having an NDE, NDA, or NLE knows one thing for sure: the experience is real. It cannot be proven empirically, but empirical science is not needed when the event has already been "proven" beyond any shadow of a doubt to the one who experienced it. The lack of scientific proof of the experiences recounted within these pages remains a stumbling block for a skeptical postindustrial society, where "knowledge" is only that which can be verified. The result of valuing empirical knowledge over and above any other, according to Seyyed Hossein Nasr, is that all knowledge becomes "desacralized." Nasr pleads for society to accept equally the experiences that can be proven scientifically and the experiences that are sacred and, so far, unprovable.[7] Nasr need not carry his plea to those who have experienced an NDE, NDA, or NLE. They know what is real and what is not.

The feelings we experience upon hearing the national anthem and seeing the nation's flag fly at full mast in the midst of skyrocketing fireworks—the tingling up and down the spine, the choking back of tears—are all part of what Gabriel Almond and Sidney Verba refer to as the "affective orientation" to one's "civic culture."[8] These automatic, deeply felt responses are also due to what Jung claimed to be the collective unconscious: behaviors and orientations we engage in without thinking; mannerisms, feelings, and traditions that we commit ourselves to without question. Yet there is a reason for doing what we do. There is a history that we may be completely unaware of. There is a call that we do not "hear" with our conscious ear. Subconsciously, however, we hear that call as clearly as a foghorn in the night.

As the dying slip ever further into a state of diminished consciousness; as the twilight moment extends its duration for the one who is engaged in journaling; as diminished consciousness increases, and a dream state increases as well; and while the bereaved focus intensely on the lost loved one, it is conceivable that one is drawn closer to a connection with the collective unconscious and to realizing an awareness never before obtained.

Perhaps a clearer way to understand how this phenomenon works, how the collective unconscious may become transparent to us, is to consider Jung's notion of the psychic system, which is composed of strata of consciousness.[9] The "topsoil" of this layered system is the individual (the ego and personal unconscious); next is the Family followed by the tribe, the nation, the ethnic group, the primitive human ancestors, and finally the animal ancestors. Flowing up and through each of these strata is a central energy that may well be the energy of the twilight moment and the power of diminished consciousness: a state of mind and consciousness that permits one to enter realms of one's past, one's ancestral roots, and pathways never before dreamed of.

It is the central energy that one taps into, whether it is by way of a twilight moment, a near-death experience, a nearing death awareness, or a near–life experience. This is how:

- My father and I were able to connect.
- So many people who are dying connect with loved ones gone before them.
- So many people who came so close to death encountered deceased loved ones.
- So many bereaved experience the presence of their deceased loved ones.
- Dawn was able to connect with her Native American ancestors.
- Jack and Greg were able to sing and speak in the language of a nation they knew so little about.
- Annie was able to fly with the animals.

As we stand vigil at the bedside of the dying, we are standing in an especially sacred space. And we invariably stand to learn something new about our God. The language of the dying is so rich in metaphor, so packed with divine meaning, that it expresses knowledge beyond anything we are normally aware of. The dying are coming to know their God, and we are a cloud of witnesses on this side while they are journeying to the cloud of witnesses on the other side. We may not be able to grasp the vision as the dying do, but they do teach us over and over again that there is another dimension to reality. And we learn that we just have to wait our turn to glimpse and hear what the dying see and hear and to grab on to what has already become theirs.

THE SPIRITUAL CONNECTION

*Do you not know that you are the temple of God,
and that the Spirit of God dwells in you?*

1 CORINTHIANS 3:16

While it may be difficult for most of us to completely internalize the notion that God dwells within each one of us, it is always easier for us to accept the idea that God dwells within others whom we deem more worthy than ourselves. But anyone who has stood at the bedside of the dying knows that the indwelling of the Spirit of God bursts forth and takes up residence in the hearts and souls of those standing vigil. To be at the bedside of any dying person is to experience a moment of divine intervention; to be at the bedside of someone we love who is dying is to come as close as is possible in this life to experiencing God's love.

What is more difficult is the acceptance that the spirits of our ancestors, ancestors never known, also dwell within us. The Native Peoples, however, are well tuned to the indwelling of the spirit of all life granted by the Great Spirit. When one is brought up to see that one's God creates all things as sacred—the winged, the four legged, the fishes, even the rocks, the hills, and the rivers—then it is a natural step to understand how the spirit of God and the ancestors dwell within us all.

If, as Richard J. Hauser, S.J., argues in his book, *Moving in the Spirit: Becoming a Contemplative in Action,* the "unitive way" is the ultimate spiritual stage in one's life journey to one's God where "advanced contemplation" is the highest quality of prayer, then it may be argued that the vast majority of those who are dying gradually have reached some measure of the unitive way.[10] Those who will listen to the stories of the dying are spiritual directors, accompanying and at times guiding those who are at the last crossroad of life. Those who listen to the dying are like air controllers who are called upon by lost or lonely pilots to hear where they are and to call them in when conditions are right.

QUESTIONS FOR REFLECTION AND DISCUSSION

How do I feel about the idea that the Spirit of God dwells within me? Do I really believe it?

How comfortable am I with Jung's idea of the psychic system? Does it end at the strata of the family? The tribe? The nation? The ethnic group? The primitive human ancestors? The animal ancestors?

What have I learned from any of my own near-death, near-life, or twilight experiences?

CHAPTER 10

~

hearing aids: engaging in the

conversation

*W*hat do all of these stories and reflections really mean to family, friends, and caregivers (professional and paraprofessional)? What do they mean to those in ministry: priest, minister, rabbi, shaman, eucharistic minister, Stephen Minister, professional counselor, and paraprofessional? What do they mean to the one who is dying? To the one who is grieving? And what do they mean to a society that is forever birthing, dying, and grieving? We might even ask, What do they mean to our God?

Marcus Borg makes the claim that "as an image of God, Jesus mirrors the care of God for what happens to humans in the world of history itself. The life of culture matters to God." [1] Furthermore, according to Borg, this God, "the compassionate one," extends an invitation to us all to enter into "a relationship, which is the source of transformation of human life in both its individual and social aspects."

The depth of one's spirituality becomes most manifest as one approaches the end of life. In a sense, death is the great equalizer. Whether we are faithfully committed to the life of our church, "pillars" of the church, daily communicants, or have not darkened the doors of any church in a lifetime, death and dying bring us all into a relationship with our God, whoever that God may be to us. It is a relationship that needs to be discussed in order that the dying and the bereaved might reveal who their God is to them and revel in that relationship.

In the end, there is very little we can do *for* the dying. We can make them comfortable, but we cannot cure that which is taking their life. There is much, however, that we can do *with* the dying. We can listen to their quest for redemption. In doing so, we play a strategic role in the dying person's and/or the bereaved's effort to find redemption. As we listen to the stories and the struggles, we are coconspirators with the people of God who seek the understanding that enlightens their faith and leads to redemptive revelation.

The Catholic Church proclaims its belief in the "redemptive death" of Jesus. It is our faith in Christ's redemptive sacrifice for us all and our faith in the Resurrection that enable us to believe that death is not the end.[2] Pierre Teilhard de Chardin describes in his essay "The Heart of Matter" how he worked out his own sense of redemption through an ongoing and developing understanding of what a devotion to the "sacred heart of Jesus" meant for him. In the end he claims to have become "engaged in making my home" in the notion of a "universal Christ" through whom redemption is available to all, for surely "God is also the Heart of All."[3]

Eastern religions offer some of the same sense of redemptive possibilities. Sogyal Rinpoche, for example, speaks of the "heart practice"—a form of meditation and prayer that focuses on the teachings of a master (such as a guru, Buddha, or Jesus) and the relationship between those teachings and one's life.[4] It is through persistent "heart practice" that one finds one's center, a sense of peace, a sense of wholeness, a sense of holiness, and a sense of being at one with the divine.

It is not the purpose here to engage in a discourse on comparative religions and their treatment of redemption. Rather, the point is to suggest that when working with a person who is dying or grieving—whether a churchgoer, Catholic, Protestant, Jew, Buddhist, Muslim, atheist, or agnostic—the very best we can do for that person is to be with him or her and to listen. At these critical times, preaching and teaching, unless requested by the dying person or the bereaved, only tend to aggravate the pain.

HOW TO LISTEN TO THE DYING OR THE BEREAVED

Some principles apply across the board, when we are trying to be good listeners at the bedside of the dying.

Begin where the person is.

Begin with that person's stories and concerns. The truck driver, Val, took the decision out of my hands. She made it rather clear where she was with the very presence of a chaplain inside her front door. "What do you want?" she asked. Until that question could be answered to her satisfaction, the chaplain would never have gotten his beer. Beginning with what people most need to talk about may well be the only thing worth discussing. Annie needed to share her near-death experience of "flying with the animals." To avoid this issue would have trivialized Annie's profound experience in the Alaskan forest.

Listen nonjudgmentally, with an ear tuned to symbolic language.

If we had been judgmental in listening to Dawn's visions of the people on the bus, the Ritual People, the Ritual Planner, the "man with the moustache," and the various colored flags, not only would her experiences have been devalued but we would also have been deprived of the wisdom her visions provided. Many times I have heard people say that someone in their past had "hallucinations" of people appearing around their beds before they died, but they kept that person grounded in reality and never heard anything more about it. People who are actively dying have little energy to protest, argue, or explain; in fact, there is no explanation available to them. In the face of others' disbelief and negative reactions, withdrawal is often the only recourse available.

Listen actively by repeating back or paraphrasing what the person says.

Val commented, "You know, I drove into and out of many terminals in my day. Now they tell me I'm it." At the time I was not at all sure what she meant by *it*. "They tell you you're it?"

I asked. Her response left no doubt. She was terminal. Others knew she was terminal. She knew others knew she was terminal; and she knew she was dying. One comment repeated back to her led to the answers to several important questions, answers that anyone working with the dying needs to have: 1) Does she know she is dying? 2) Does the family know? 3) Are they accepting of what they know?

Sometimes asking, "Is there more you would like to say about that?" or "How does that feel?" empowers the other person to peel away one more layer of protective covering and reveal some of the true self. However, we must keep in mind that the compelling purpose to active listening is not that we will know the dying better, but that they will better know themselves and their God.

Provide leading questions in order to engage in the conversation.

Often this is the only way to move forward, because after saying Hello, there seems to be no place to go. In those cases, one needs to ask a question or two. Margaret, bargaining cancer for three more years with her children, was particularly reticent from the beginning. "What's happening, Margaret?" seemed to unlock some of the anticipated grief incarcerated within her soul. Wanting to see her daughter graduate was a most understandable desire. Observing that it "sounds like a very important goal for you" resulted in knowing Margaret a whole lot better. Her response warned us of how difficult it would be for her to let go, even when her body was giving her no negotiating room.

Value the silence when there seems to be no place to go.
As the silence between musical notes brings out the richness of
tone and timbre, and as the negative space representing the sky
in a drawing of a mountain enhances the beauty of the mountain, so too does the silence in interpersonal communication
enhance the economy of spoken words. Indeed, the silence may
be the very essence of the conversation.

We tend, however, to be uncomfortable with silence. We
are a culture of clutter and clatter. If the television is not on,
we are lonely. If the other person is not talking, he or she must
not like us. If the radio goes silent for more than ten seconds,
we are convinced that it's gone dead. Silence is a decision to
keep one's mouth shut and to listen with the heart. Would
Annie, the Mormon missionary, have been as open to sharing
her near-death experience if her family and I had not maintained a silent vigil at her bedside? Would Steffen have opened
up to share his need for forgiveness if it were not for a vigil of
patience, presence, and silence at his bedside?

Accept as normal the person's fears and concerns.
Elissa feared that she might be seen as crazy because of her
visions of her deceased dad. "Do you think I'm crazy?" she
asked. Responding with "No, I sure don't" seemed to reassure
her. But it was the poem by John Milton that convinced her
she was okay. For the person who seems to be exhibiting signs
of the fear of dying, it is often helpful to interject: "Many
people express a fear of dying. Can you relate to that?" For the
family member who indicates a difficulty in giving the dying
person permission to go, it might be helpful to share one's own

struggle with letting go of a loved one. These are but a few ways we have of reassuring people that they are not, as Elissa put it, weird.

Allow and encourage the person to keep talking.
"Don't you see them?" Dawn asked a number of times. I would respond: "No, I don't, but your vision is different than mine these days. Why don't you just tell me about them?" In doing so, by encouraging her to say more, her visions were validated, and I became all the more aware of the many dimensions to Dawn's journey to her God. I also began a new journey of my own with an ever deepening understanding of how God is present in our living and in our dying.

Say what needs to be said, and always say good-bye.
Steffen, dying of AIDS, had an overwhelming need to say what needed to be said to a number of people in his life. But he also needed to hear what needed to be said to him. Not doing so could have made Steffen's dying harder than his living.

For health-care providers or people who minister to the terminally ill, it is helpful to say upon departing a patient's presence, even when there is no good reason to believe that death will occur before you return, "Just in case your God may call you home before I get back to see you, I want you to know how much I appreciate . . ." I have lost count of the number of times I have been glad that I said something similar to the people I have met in hospice. Similar comments give the dying person one more articulated permission to go. It also gives us a sense that we said what needed to be said.

Encourage the use of the arts as a means of processing anticipated and postdeath grief.

As noted throughout this book, the arts—whether music, film, paintings, sculpture, literature, or the art of journaling—can be effective therapy for broken hearts. There is nothing wrong with suggesting a video to a family with the comment, "I think you would really like this." We make such recommendations to our friends all the time. Why not at this time of testing and pain when people are looking for ways to make sense of the senseless?

HOW *NOT* TO LISTEN TO THE DYING OR THE BEREAVED

There are some things we should not do if we are to give real support at this critical time.

Don't assume that you know what is going on.

When Dawn gratefully acknowledged that "those people" had given her a "ticket for the bus," I could have assumed she was hallucinating and ignored her good news. Instead, even though I thought I knew where the bus was headed, I asked, "Where is the bus going?"

Dee assumed that her mother had never lost a child to death. As a result, she was terribly frightened when her mother pleaded for the deceased infant to come to her. The truth set Dee free. The truth allowed Dee to set her mother free.

Don't argue with the dying.

Marian's daughters tried to argue with her. No, she was not going to go anywhere. But they soon learned that she knew exactly where she was going and that Dad was going to help her get there.

Yes, Duncan *had* sold the horses; but when he told Marilou to hitch them up, he knew it was time to go. No amount of arguing could change that fact. Often we think that the dying person is confused. It is not the dying, but the rest of us, who are confused.

Don't prejudge, judge, deny, or discount what the patient knows to be true.

Sonny denied that Granny could possibly have seen his father that day. His father was dead, but Granny, fortunately, ignored her grandson's denial and went on to explain that his deceased dad had come back to build her a shed to put her stuff in. Granny knew it was time for her to pack up and go to her God. Granny also turned a deaf ear to Earl's claim that she was not going to die, that she had a lot of years left.

If Ruth Anne Dodge's family had denied that she could possibly see an angel in the prow of a boat, the statue of the Black Angel would not exist to testify to the symbolic language of the dying.

Don't preach or shift into problem solving with a dying person or with the bereaved.

Usually, the dying and the bereaved just need someone to listen to them. Even when questions are raised regarding the omissions and commissions of life, neither the dying nor the bereaved are looking to doctors, lawyers, priests, rabbis, shamans, gurus, or chaplains for the answers. The answers lie within themselves. "What do you think?" is the preferred therapeutic response, rather than "What I think is . . ." On the other hand, if the answer seems hopelessly locked up, then it is time to move into a more intentional mode of "brief pastoral counseling" or refer the person to long-term counseling.[5]

Don't hold out false hope or hang on to the patient.
Mary's family hung on for a very long time, offering her much unfounded hope. St. Martin de Tours's brother monks pleaded with him to not leave them. As much as we love the dying, we must let them know that it is okay to go. After our loved one is gone, we will have many moments in which we are called upon again to let go. Hanging on to the person who is dying only prolongs both the dying and the grieving processes; it does little or nothing to prolong that person's quality of life.

THE SPIRITUAL CONNECTION

"Anyone who has ears to hear ought to hear." He also told them, "Take care what you hear."

MARK 4:23–24

Know this . . . be quick to hear [and] slow to speak.

JAMES 1:19

Before hearing, answer not,
and interrupt no one in the middle of his speech.

SIRACH 11:8

To listen attentively to the dying and the grieving is to listen to God. To be present at the bedside of one of God's human creatures at the time of death is to stand on holy ground. To listen to the bereaved is to be only slightly removed from that same holy ground, for the bereaved bring the ground with them. For that holiest of reasons, we must listen carefully to the words of those who are dying and those who are trying to relearn their way.

As James and Sirach point out, we must be quick to hear and keep our mouths shut, for at these precious moments we may well reside in a time and space that are full of the promise and presence of God. The time of death is a quiet time, often eerie in its stillness. The time of bereavement can be equally quiet, filled with silent wailing and dry tears. We who journey with the dying and the bereaved find ourselves in a space somehow set apart from the rest of the world. Nothing else matters except for you, Thou, and I.

The space we are in is sacred space. Do we desecrate that holy space with the pollutant of our words, or do we join Elijah in his cave of mourning on Mt. Horeb (1 Kings 19:9–13)? We, like Elijah, look for the Lord in the strong winds of testing and pain, but we may not find the Lord there. We, like Elijah, look for the Lord in the frightening earthquakes, tornadoes, and hurricanes of life gone berserk. But we may not find him there. We, like Elijah, look for the Lord in the fires that seem to consume everything. But we may not find him there.

Yet, like Elijah, we can stand in the quiet cave of the dying and the grieving and come to know that we have experienced the Divine in "a tiny whispering sound." And so, we join Elijah by hiding our faces. We stand "at the entrance of the cave" saying, "Amen. Amen". When the voice of God asks us, "Why are you here?" we know beyond the shadow of a doubt that we came to witness the miracles and wonders of a loving God who "will guard your coming and going,/both now and forever" (Ps. 121:8).

QUESTIONS FOR REFLECTION AND DISCUSSION

For me, the best experience of being listened to was when . . .

The best job of listening I ever did was when . . .

I heard the "tiny whispering sound" of God when . . .

CHAPTER ELEVEN

—➤

learning from the dying

*t*o be at the bedside of a person who is dying is like learning from the perfect tutor. Sometimes the wisdom comes to us in very clear and concise language. Sometimes it is a coded knowledge, and we do the deciphering later. Sometimes the learning is direct and even stark, if not startling. Other times it is subtle and quite mystifying. Sometimes we learn by listening; other times, we learn by watching.

But always, if we are open to the moment and to the person who is dying, we learn something about living and about dying. The dying rarely have the energy to teach us intentionally. We who stand on the sidelines are the ones who need to raise the questions: "What am I learning here? What am I being taught? What is the wisdom being left behind by this person right now?" The question never is, "Is there even anything to be learned here?" The only real question is, "What is the wisdom being shared with me as I stand the vigil?"

We can find ourselves in an Ivy League college with a world-class instructor and learn nothing because of our own lack of openness. If we think all of the answers are in, if we do not believe this person has anything more to say, then we learn nothing from the Mildred Klinghofers in our lives:

> In the last hours when her mind wandered, she cried imperiously,
> "My baby! give me my baby!"
> And her cries for this child, born of her mind,
> in her final moments of life, went on and on.
> When they answered, "Your baby isn't here" or
> "Your baby is coming soon if you will wait,"
> she kept on with her cry,
> "My baby! let me hold my baby!"
>
> CARL SANDBURG,
> "THE PEOPLE, YES #8"[1]

We do not know for sure, of course, but one read of these lines is that Mildred died actually seeing one of her deceased infants, for it is noted earlier: "One baby came and was taken away, another came and was taken away." Perhaps like Sheila (chapter four), Mildred's vision was much more than the dream Sandburg presumed as he wrote how they placed a doll in Mildred's arms:

And she was satisfied and her second childhood ended
like her first, with a doll in her arms.
There are dreams stronger than death.
Men and women die holding these dreams.

While not wanting to deny that we may die holding our dreams, it seems quite likely in the case of Mildred Klinghofer that she died in the presence of her infants, who had come to take her home. By arguing with Mildred and denying her reality, those present missed an opportunity to learn something.

One of the things we learn quite readily from the dying is that dying is not easy. When we see a person looking vibrantly alive one day, who is then diagnosed with terminal illness after a routine physical examination and then dies a week later, the process may appear simple and quick, especially when compared to the prolonged ravages of Alzheimer's or Huntington's chorea. Yet the process is never easy. Physical, psychological, emotional, and spiritual pains are often part and parcel of the dying process as much as fluctuating blood pressure and decreasing strength.

Some of the other things we learn from walking with the dying are that their bodies tell them a great deal. The dying are the first to know when the time has come. We learn too that the dying have a profound need to know that their loved ones will be okay after they go. The dying have an equally profound need to hear from those they love that it is okay to go. As we have seen over and over again in this book, the dying are not alone even when we think they are alone. What may not be quite so clear is that the process of dying has everything to do with the process of living.

The focal point of this chapter is on the need for being attentive to what we can learn from the dying as they repeatedly and almost predictably demonstrate to us how

1. No one dies alone.
2. We die the way we live.
3. Reflected fear stalls and aggravates the natural dying process.

NO ONE DIES ALONE

The many sightings related within these pages, of dying people seeing someone whom others in the room cannot see, make clear that few if any people die alone. In the words of Callanan and Kelley, "Death is not lonely. . . . Those who have died before us, or some spiritual beings, will be companions on our journey."[2] Or, as Elisabeth Kübler-Ross concludes: "In general, the people who are waiting for us on the other side are the ones who loved us the most. You always meet those people first."[3]

So often, family will hover at the bedside wanting to be sure that they are present when their loved one dies. They do not want the dying person to feel abandoned. They cannot imagine anyone wanting to die alone. But then they step out of the room to go for lunch, go for a walk, run an errand, get a drink, find the restroom, or make a telephone call, and when they return to the bedroom, the loved one has expired. Consequently, those left behind blame themselves for not being there when death occurred.

The fact is that many dying people seem to purposely let go when none of the living are in the room. Some dying people with the strength and cognizance to do so even make up excuses for their loved ones to leave the room. Whether it is due to a need to protect loved ones from witnessing the final breath or a need for personal space to commit the most significant act of their lives (or both), most people die without any living beings around them. But we know for sure that loved ones who have already made the journey are there to ease the way.

One time, after I had given a presentation on this topic, a young mother said, "I can go home tonight and sleep, something I have not been able to do for two years." She went on to describe to me with the greatest, tearful effort how she had discovered her three-year-old daughter dead in bed one morning. Her only child had been perfectly healthy when she was put to bed the night before, but now she was dead. "I have beaten myself up, even when I knew logically that there was no way for me to have known Angie would be ill, to say nothing about dying. But I have torn myself like a shredded blanket, blaming, punishing myself for not being there. I have cried myself to sleep at night, in the morning, and in the middle of the day for the fact that Angie died alone. And now..."

This young mother, who had aged twenty years in two, stood in the middle of this church hall after everyone else had gone home just to tell me: "Now I know that Angie did not die alone. I'm sure my parents, Angie's grandparents, and my brother were right there to comfort her and to help her across."

Yes, the dying teach us that we do not die alone, but they also teach us that death is not the end. Elisabeth Kübler-Ross states succinctly how she learned this lesson from the dying:

*Before I started working with dying patients, I did not
believe in a life after death. I now do believe in a life after
death, beyond a shadow of a doubt.*[4]

WE DIE THE WAY WE LIVE

Those who have known the dying person well throughout life
have access to knowledge that can help them predict how that
person might die. They are privy to what lies ahead as this person moves closer and closer to the end. Knowing how a person
has run the race of life provides us with an inside view to how
that same person is going to finish the race. A person who
has lived a well-organized life, always concerned about the
details of family, friends, and finance, will take care of final
arrangements down to having the obituary written and dictat-
ing the funeral luncheon menu. Someone who has always been
uncomfortable with the unknown, who hates surprises and
requires constant reassurance, will die an anxious death. Those
who have always been the reconciler in life will make every
possible effort to make sure all is right before letting go. Those
who have lived a life of relative detachment will probably
die while no one is physically present.

Gabe the hermit
Gabe's life was seen by many people as the life of a hermit. He was
never married. During his working years, Gabe got out of bed
each morning, ate breakfast, went to his job as a mechanic, came
home, fixed dinner, watched television, went to bed, and got up
the next morning to repeat the cycle of his life. Those who knew

him better were quite aware that Gabe loved his nephews and nieces dearly. He enjoyed being with them for a time, but he would rarely tarry. Gabe would soon say, "Well, I need to be gittin'."

Cancer changed his life. His physician recommended that Gabe have someone with him most of the time. Gabe would not hear of it: "I can't stand folks hovering over me." Finally, he consented to hospice care, but he made one condition very clear before signing the papers: "You call before you come, do ya hear?"

Many times when the nurse would call to make an appointment, Gabe would decline a visit. It was never possible to schedule a visit even a day ahead. There were certain times during the day that were definitely off-limits to anyone, family included. These were the scheduled times for his favorite TV programs. The stories were plentiful of how he had ejected family from his small apartment because it was nearly time for one of the TV shows. Gabe protected his privacy; that did not change just because he was dying.

Early one morning the hospice nurse called Gabe. There was no answer. She waited a few minutes, thinking he might be in the bathroom, and called again. Still no answer. The nurse then called Gabe's niece, who had been checking on him regularly at night and early in the mornings. The niece had also called him and had gotten no answer; she was about to head over to her uncle's.

Niece, nurse, chaplain, and social worker all arrived at about the same time. Looking through the living room window, we could see Gabe in his easy chair in front of the television. He appeared to be asleep, but he failed to wake up when we rang the doorbell, pounded on the door, or tapped on the window.

Having no key to Gabe's home (he had refused a key even to his niece), we had no alternative but to force entry. It was then that we knew Gabe had died and had probably done so while watching his favorite early morning TV show. Gabe had led a solitary life; he died a solitary death. He lived a life of doing it his own way; he died doing it his own way as well.

Sam the magician

Sam was a magician. He had other employment as an auto-parts technician, but he saw himself primarily as a magician. He worked for hire as a magician. He traveled far and wide, sharing his magical acts on stage, in classrooms, in parish halls, in community centers, on Amtrak, and on television.

Now, however, Sam was at the point of giving up the fight against cancer. No amount of magic could rid his body of this ugly uninvited guest. There was little time left, and Sam knew it better than anyone else. He could barely speak in an audible and discernible fashion. There was nothing that he could do for and by himself—or so it seemed.

A friend stopped by to see Sam. As the friend entered the room, Sam spoke very softly, beckoning with one finger for the friend to come closer. Finally, standing at Sam's bedside, the friend was beckoned to come even closer.

"Watch me," whispered Sam to his friend. "Watch me real close. You're about to see the greatest act of all."

Sam's friend carefully watched, at first not realizing what he was seeing. Soon, it dawned on him that despite Sam's broad smile and his eyes being wide open, Sam was dead. He had performed his greatest act. Sam had lived a life of performing some rather spectacular acts, but this was the most spectacular of all. As a magician, Sam was always in control of his act. Nothing had changed.

If dying can ever be a happy event, these are happy stories. Sometimes dying, however, is far from being a happy event. The stories that follow are not happy stories, primarily because they are conclusions to lives that were far from happy.

Jake the gambler

Jake was a gambler. He gambled on everything from lottery cards to dogs at the track, football, one-armed bandits, and blackjack at the casinos. Jake was a loser as a gambler. He had lost his first wife, who could no longer endure his addiction or the perpetual hounding by collection agents.

Jake gambled on good health getting him to his long-held goal of reaching a hundred. Unfortunately, he lost that gamble by forty years. He gambled on chemo beating the cancer but lost that bet when the oncologist concluded that any further treatments were pointless.

Upon entering Jake's home for the first time, I immediately took note of the barrenness of the place: one lamp, one shabby couch, and no chairs in the entire house. Jake had lost nearly every possession to the collection agencies. Jake, however, had not yet folded his hand.

He insisted day after day that someone must take him to the casino. Family members tried to reason with him that he no longer had the strength to even be wheeled into the casino. It had been days now since he had eaten. He was strictly on liquids and was losing weight each day. Yet this emaciated man kept insisting with increasing agitation and anger, "Take me to the casino. God damn it, I want to go to the casino. Do you people hear me?"

Finally, a son-in-law agreed to take him with the understanding that they would just drive by. Jake seemed to be fine with that. But as they drove onto the casino grounds, Jake, who had been silent so far, suddenly began demanding that he be taken into the casino.

"But Dad, remember we agreed just to do a drive-by."

"Damn it all, then drop me off. I'll call ya when I'm ready to come home."

Pete kept driving, coming closer and closer to the main entrance. Suddenly, Jake managed to open the passenger door. Pete instinctively stopped the car. Jake threw himself out of the car, landing on the asphalt. Jake now had a broken arm and bruises on his forehead.

Jake died three days later. He had gambled on one last trip to the casino before he cashed in his chips.

Bart the abuser

Things were not going well. Bart's daughter, who was trying to raise her family, maintain her full-time job, and care for her father, had called to vent some of her feelings to our social worker. Her voice was filled with burnout and fatigue. The social worker and I decided we would make a visit in order to assess the situation.

As we stepped out of the car on that beautiful summer day, we could hear Bart's angry voice resounding from inside the house. It was not a pretty sound: "Damn you. Damn you all. When I get out of this bed I'm going to beat the shit outta you, girl."

We wondered if the daughter could hear the doorbell over this diatribe. Finally, Carla came to the door. She was crying.

"Is this new behavior?" I asked.

Carla laughed a bitter laugh. "Hardly. Actually this is pretty normal."

We entered this troubled home and went directly to Bart's bedside. While he was civil to the "hospice people," Bart was far from civil to his daughter even with the "hospice people" present. He had a unique command of a vocabulary limited almost exclusively to four-letter words. He referred to Carla with offensive epithets; not once did he call her by name. Every effort to communicate with this patient was met with sullen silence.

As we walked out to the car, the social worker observed, "It isn't easy, is it?"

Carla began to cry with pent-up anger. "You don't know how hard it is to be caring for a man I hate with every ounce of energy I have." She went on to explain that her father raped her mother on their first date and had finally married her only under duress. Throughout her life as the oldest child, Carla had witnessed her mother being abused. Carla's brother, who had moved far away, refused to come visit his father. He promised to come only "after the son of a bitch dies, so that I can flush his ashes down the toilet where he belongs."

Carla's oldest child was her father's. "He has sexually abused each one of my three kids. I hate the bastard," Carla screamed as she turned toward the house, aiming her pain straight through the walls.

Within two days, Carla's agony lessened. Bart became unconscious. He was no longer able to abuse those around him. He died three days after slipping into the coma. But up to the point of losing consciousness, Bart continued his abusive life by dying an abusive death.

REFLECTED FEAR STALLS AND AGGRAVATES THE NATURAL DYING PROCESS

Often, the dying are held in bondage by the fears of their loved ones. A daughter going through a bitter divorce hangs on to her dying mother, refusing to let go of her lifeline. To lose her mother is to lose the one sure thing in her life. A husband who knows that his wife is dying refuses to acknowledge the "worse prognosis," for to do otherwise would mean that he would need to begin preparing himself for life without her. To lose his wife is to lose the one who has always been there for him.

Unfortunately, sometimes when the body is on the brink of death, the dying person does not yet feel free to go. He or she cannot let go, because others are not yet ready to let go. As a rule, we hang on to our loved ones not for their sake, but for ours.

I thought I had reached a point of acceptance of Dawn's dying. I had told her that she need not continue doing treatments for my sake. Later on, I was praying that God would take her soon, that the suffering would end. I asked friends to pray not for her healing anymore but for the Lord to spare her any more pain and to take her home. But one day in the final week of her life, she said, "People need to let me go."

"Who?" I asked, thinking she would mention one or more of our children.

"You." She looked me straight in the eye. She had picked up on my fears of being alone, of no longer having her in my life. My fears were being reflected in my eyes, the tone of my voice, and my constant attention to her. I knew she was right. I had said all the right words, but in my heart I was still clinging to the love of my life. At that moment I also knew beyond any shadow of a doubt that Dawn was ready to go; she needed to go; the bus was coming, and I needed to step aside.

She died a few days later.

"We don't know why she is still alive!"
One morning the director of nursing at a hospital in our service area called, apparently hoping to unload a problem. A woman in her late eighties was lying in a near coma after having fought an extensive battle with cancer for seven years. The physician had informed the family that there was nothing more he could do. The husband wanted to do more testing and treatment on the advice of their physician son, who lived some distance away. The nurse informed us that the patient's physician was "at his wit's end" with the family. The patient would probably die within the next few days. "Is there anything you can do to help us with this family?"

Without knowing what we could possibly do in this case, our social worker, a nurse, and I jumped into the car and drove the sixty miles to the hospital. Given the nurse's assessment, it sounded as if we were dealing with reflected fear: a patient hanging on to life only because she was afraid to let go and leave a terrified family behind. Perhaps if the family could accept her dying, she could relax and go meet her God.

As we walked into the room, I noticed that the patient, Mary, was lying with eyes closed. Her spouse, Frank, and a family friend were at either side of her bed. Frank quickly explained: "We are going to do some more tests to see if we can beat this thing."

He was a big man, a person who obviously knew what work was. He had gnarled hands, a gnarled face, and was dressed to return to the fields. From what little I knew it was safe to assume that this hardworking farmer had been through a great deal with his spouse. Frank was a fighter and a survivor. He was not a quitter.

"Is that what Mary wants?" I asked.

"Well, I don't know. She has never said, but maybe I wasn't listening."

"That may be, but would you be ready to listen to her now?"

Frank cupped his face with his hand and rubbed his jaw and cheekbone repeatedly, looking at the floor, then to Mary, and back to the floor. He seemed to be searching for an answer.

Finally, Frank's eyes connected with mine, and what I saw startled me. I was peering into the depths of an anguished soul. Tears were welling in the eyes of a human being I judged had rarely allowed himself to grieve, especially in the presence of other people.

"You don't know how much comfort it would be to me to know what she really wants us to do," Frank said. He was looking at Mary, whose eyes were now open. "But it's too late. She can't talk. She doesn't understand what's going on. It's just too late!" This silver-haired man, so accustomed to taking charge, making decisions, solving problems, but worn down with seven years of treatments, tests, and torment, was sitting now with his head down, chin to his chest, quietly sobbing.

I didn't quite know what to do, but said, "There are different ways to communicate, and I would like to try to talk with Mary. My question is, Are you ready to hear what she may say she wants?" Frank slowly lifted his head and said in a weak, defeated voice, "Yes."

Encouraging everyone to come to the bedside, I took Mary's hand and spoke to her: "Do you hear me, Mary?" There was a slight change in the expression of her eyes, and I sensed that she probably did hear me. "Mary, we need to make some decisions, but Frank needs to know what you want to do. If you understand, squeeze Frank's hand." For what felt like an eternity, we waited for the squeeze. Finally, Frank told me he could feel nothing.

"Mary, if you understand what I have said, blink your eyes." Without hesitation, Mary blinked her eyes and smiled.

"Mary, if you want to continue the fight; if you want to beat this thing; if you want some more tests and treatment, then blink your eyes once."

Mary just stared. I wondered if I had misread her blink and smile. Was her smile our very last connection with this dying person? Had we arrived too late to "hear" Mary?

"Mary, we are trying to read your eyes. If you have the energy for it, please blink your eyes twice to let us know you understand. Can you do that?" Immediately, her eyes blinked twice in rapid succession and she smiled. Now I knew we could do this.

"Mary, if you want no further tests and treatments; if you want to give up the battle against the cancer; if you want to go on to your God; if you want Frank and the family to let you go, blink your eyes once." Instantly, Mary's eyes closed in an intense and protracted blink.

Frank's huge frame sagged. He searched for a chair to hold his body together as his soul dealt with all that had been avoided, all that had been feared, all that had really been known but denied, all that had ever been, and all that would never be again.

In a blink of her eyes Mary finally had the chance to settle the issue. She finally regained control of her life and control of her dying. In the blink of an eye, a determined and denying family came to a level of acceptance. As we prayed together with Mary, there appeared to be a near total trust in the providence of God. Mary died very peacefully six hours later. It was as if Jesus had said to Frank's Mary, "Go in peace and be cured of your affliction" (Mark 5:34).

THE SPIRITUAL CONNECTION

Dying was not easy for Jesus. He knew he was dying as he stood in the Garden of Gethsemane. It was here, according to Mark, that Jesus "began to be troubled and distressed" (Mark 14:33). Jesus turned to his disciples and said, "My soul is sorrowful even to death" (Mark 14:34). Then, there was the humiliation and the pain of all that led up to being nailed to the cross. Finally, from the cross itself Jesus was heard to cry out, "'Eloi, Eloi, lema sabachthani?' which is translated, 'My God, my God, why have you forsaken me?'" (Mark 15:34)

Jesus' death was as difficult as it gets. We know for sure that he suffered physically, emotionally, and spiritually to the point

LEARNING FROM THE DYING

of feeling abandoned even by his Father. When it comes time for each one of us to die, we too will carry our cross, and it will not be easy. We too may find our hearts filled with fear and distress. We too may feel as if we have been forsaken. We can hope, however, that we will hear Jesus saying, "Go in peace, and be free from this illness."

May the experiences shared here make death and dying easier to handle when it comes time to cope with our own dying or with the dying of those we love. If it helps to know that no one dies alone, that death is not the end, and that there is some kind of reality beyond death itself, then perhaps we can see that life is not an end in and of itself. Perhaps we can welcome death with a little less fear, distress, and sorrow. Maybe that is part of what Jesus died for: to help us cope with our own final act.

Jesus is the perfect tutor in living our lives and dying our deaths. As he hung on the cross he was able to proclaim his readiness to let go: "Father, into your hands I commend my spirit" (Luke 23:46). Marian and Granny (chapter two) are two people who were seemingly able to say the same to their God. Will we be able to follow suit when our time comes?

Jesus also died the way he lived. He comforted the hurting and forgave sins as he lived. He carried that same behavior to the cross as he spoke words of consolation to those condemned and hanging on crosses on the same hill. Steffen and Alvin in chapter six were able to demonstrate how forgiveness works in the daily life of the dying.

QUESTIONS FOR REFLECTION AND DISCUSSION

What dreams will I be holding when I die?

Given how I live my life, how will I be when I face my own dying?

How does a close inspection of Jesus' experience with dying help me to understand the nature of dying as a process?

afterword

~

When a loved one dies, we are left behind and alone in our grief. There may be plenty of people willing to listen to us and help as they can, but grieving is like being alone in a crowd. There are bereavement support groups available to help us process the grief, but no one can do it for us. It may even seem that we are in a catch-22, where the one person who could help more than any other is gone forever.

The intensity and duration of grieving varies in direct proportion to the depth and importance of the lost physical relationship. Two people in relationship are like two intersecting circles. The more intimate the relationship, the deeper the intersection. If we could illustrate the resulting relationship, it would be that portion of the overlapping circles.

If we colored the overlap purple, we would have a graphic glimpse at the magnitude of the grief task that lies ahead for the person left behind. Yet the color purple also represents the well of memory that we can draw upon to refresh us as we travel the sometimes arid terrain of grief and grieving.

We may feel as if the one who died has abandoned us and left us to cope with no resources other than our memories. But it is in our memories that we can find the key to healing the heartache of loss. The very notion of memory comes, in part, from the Old Norse term *mimir,* meaning "a giant who guards the well of wisdom."[1] Memory is truly the giant who guards the wisdom of the past, the present, and the future.

Grief, according to Molly Fumia, is "the process of exhuming all that has been, examining its precious contents, and lovingly preparing it for reburial."[2] Our well of wisdom is stocked with memories of the person who has gone.

Reflecting upon the special moments, pouring over photo albums, journaling about a loved one, and revisiting the special places mutually valued are some of the ways we have of "exhuming all that has been."

Recalling how a loved one may have talked about visitors unseen by us, noting how the loved one seemed to be at peace with his or her dying, and being ready (if not eager) to go are a few ways of "examining [the] precious contents" of our grief.

Knowing that a loved one did not die alone, even when she or he expired with no earthly being at the bedside; realizing that we did all we could do; noting that all of us were able to let go; recounting how the person whom we so loved died exactly the way she had lived; having passionately experienced the holiness of the ground upon which we stood while at his bedside; and gratefully acknowledging that death is not the end are but a few of the ways we have of "lovingly preparing [our grief] for reburial."

Thomas Attig's understanding of the grieving process fleshes out our awareness of the dynamics and nature of the reburial process. As Attig views the matter, grieving the loss of a very significant person in our lives forces us into a situation where we need to learn all over again how to function in and relate to a world that no longer includes that other person.[3]

All of a sudden we must relearn the very world around us. So much of our world is defined through the existence of a significant other. When that person leaves our life, much of the world as we know it also leaves. Thus, we discover that so much of our notion of who we are has also been defined by that other person's presence. With that person's death comes a need to redefine who we are. Grieving then, according to Attig, requires a process of learning all over again how to relate to everything and everyone in our world. It also requires a relearning of our relationship with the deceased person as well. All of this relearning takes time—a lifetime.

But we hope that, as we reach the end of our own lifetime, we will have learned from the loved ones gone before us how to "do it right." Let us pray that by listening well to the dying, we may learn how to catch the bus marked *Heaven Bound*.

notes

Chapter One

1. Elisabeth Kübler-Ross, "On Life after Death," in *On Death and Dying* (New York: Macmillan, 1991), 60.

Chapter Two

1. *Shadowlands* (Worcester, Pa.: Gateway Films Vision V Video, 1985, BBC).

2. *A Family Thing* (Santa Monica, Calif.: MGM/UA Home Video, 1995, United Artists).

3. Kübler-Ross, "On Life after Death," 60.

Chapter Three

1. Elisabeth Kübler-Ross, *Death: The Final Stage of Growth* (New York: Simon & Schuster, 1986), and *On Death and Dying* (cf 2, preface); Melvin Morse with Paul Perry, *Transformed by the Light: The Powerful Effect of Near-Death Experiences on People's Lives* (New York: Villard Books, 1992); Raymond A. Moody, *Life after Life: The Investigation of a Phenomenon—Survival of Bodily Death* (Harrisburg, Pa.: Stackpole Books, 1976).

2. Morse, *Transformed by the Light,* 6–189.

Chapter Four

1. Maggie Callanan and Patricia Kelley, *Final Gifts: Understanding the Special Awareness, Needs, and Communications of the Dying* (New York: Poseidon 1992).

2. Sogyal Rinpoche, *The Tibetan Book of Living and Dying,* ed. Patrick Gaffney and Andrew Harvey (San Francisco: HarperSanFrancisco, 1992), 284.

3. Scott Slater and Alec Solomita, *Exits: Stories of Dying Moments amd Parting Words* (New York: Dutton, 1980), 5.

4. Ibid., 19.

5. Milton Cross and David Ewen, *Encyclopedia of the Great Composers and Their Music,* New rev. ed. (Garden City, N.Y.: Doubleday, 1962), 603.

6. Ibid., 802.

7. *The Liturgy of the Hours: According to the Roman Rite,* vol. 4 (New York: Catholic Book Publishing, 1975), 8. Ibid. 1552-53.

8. Ibid.

9. Robert Bly, "Third Body," in *Loving a Woman in Two Worlds* (New York: Perennial Library, 1987), 19.

10. Dietrich Bonhoeffer, *The Cost of Discipleship,* trans. R. H. Fuller (New York: Macmillan, 1959), 35ff.

Chapter Five

1. William Carlos Williams, *The Doctor Stories,* comp. by Robert Coles (New York: New Directions, 1984), 123–26.

2. *The Ruth Anne Dodge Memorial* at Fairview Cemetery, Council Bluffs, Iowa.

3. Kübler-Ross, "On Life after Death," 60.

Chapter Six

1. Hannah Arendt, *The Human Condition* (Chicago: University of Chicago Press, 1958), 239.

2. John Tarrant, *The Light inside the Dark: Zen, Soul, and the Spiritual Life* (New York: HarperCollins, 1998), 13.

3. *The Straight Story* (Burbank, Calif.: Walt Disney Home Video, 1999).

4. An adaptation of an article previously published by this author entitled "Learning Forgiveness from an AIDS Patient," *VISION* (October 1998), 19.

5. Tory Dent, "HIV, Mon Amour #XIX," in *HIV, Mon Amour: Poems* (Riverdale-on-Hudson, N.Y.: Sheep Meadow, 1999), 77.

Chapter Seven

1. Madeleine L'Engle, *Walking on Water: Reflections on Faith and Art* (Wheaton, Ill.: Harold Shaw Publishers, 1980), 45–46.

2. Black Elk, *The Sacred Pipe: Black Elk's Account of the Seven Rites of the Oglala Sioux,* recorded and edited by Joseph Epes Brown (Norman, Okla.: University of Oklahoma Press, 1953).

3. William K. Powers, *Oglala Religion* (Lincoln, Nebr.: University of Nebraska Press, 1977).

4. John G. Neihardt, *Black Elk Speaks* (New York: MJF Books, 1996).

5. Powers, 103.

6. Ibid., 100.

7. Ibid., 100.

8. William Stolzman, *The Pipe and Christ* (Chamberlain, S.D.: Tipi, 1991), 78.

9. Ibid., 148.

10. Powers, 165.

11. Stolzman, 140.

12. Ira Progoff, *At a Journal Workshop: The Basic Text and Guide for Using the Intensive Journal Process* (New York: Dialogue House Library, 1975).

13. Matthew 17:1–8; Mark 9:2–9; Luke 9:28–36; or 2 Peter 1:16–18.

14. Cf. Mark 9:2–8.

Chapter Eight

1. *Field of Dreams* (Universal City, Calif.: MCA Universal Home Video, 1989).

2. *Ghost* (Hollywood, Calif.: Paramount Pictures, 1990).

3. *Sleepless in Seattle* (Burbank, Calif.: Columbia Tristar Home Video, 1993).

4. John Milton, "On His Deceased Wife," in *The Top 500 Poems,* ed. William Harmon (New York: Columbia University, 1992), 209.

5. *The Liturgy of the Hours,* vol. 3, 1372-73.

6. *The American Heritage Dictionary of the English Language: New College Edition* (Boston: Houghton Mifflin, 1980), 1548, S.V. *Vision*

7. Evelyn Underhill, *Mixed Pasture; Twelve Essays and Addresses* (New York: Methuen, 1933), 9.

8. Eddie Ensley, *Visions: The Soul's Path to the Sacred* (Chicago: Loyola Press, 2000), 232.

Chapter Nine

1. Jolande Székács Jacobi, *The Psychology of C. G. Jung: An Introduction with Illustrations,* trans. Ralph Manheim (New Haven, Conn.: Yale University Press, 1962), 149.

2. Ibid., 33.

3. Ibid., 85.

4. Progoff, *At a Journal Workshop,* 77-85.

5. Ibid., 81.

6. Ira Progoff, *Jung, Synchronicity, and Human Destiny: C. G. Jung's Theory of Meaningful Coincidence* (New York: Dialogue House Library, 1975), 83.

7. Seyyed Hossein Nasr, *Knowledge and the Sacred* (New York: Crossroad, 1981), 1–64.

8. Gabriel A. Almond and Sidney Verba, *The Civic Culture: Political Attitudes and Democracy in Five Nations, an Analytic Study* (Boston: Little, Brown, 1965), 14.

9. Jacobi, 73.

10. Richard J. Hauser, *Moving in the Spirit: Becoming a Contemplative in Action* (New York: Paulist, 1986), 13–21.

Chapter Ten

1. Marcus J. Borg, *Jesus, a New Vision: Spirit, Culture, and the Life of Discipleship* (San Francisco: Harper & Row, 1987), 192.

2. *Catechism of the Catholic Church* (New York: William H. Sadlier, 1994), 146, 258.

3. Pierre Teilhard de Chardin, *The Heart of Matter,* trans. René Hague (New York: Harcourt Brace Jovanovich, 1979), 44, 66.

4. Rinpoche, 144–49, 313–315.

5. Howard Stone, *Brief Pastoral Counseling: Short-Term Approach and Strategies* (Fortress Press, 1994).

Chapter Eleven

1. Carl Sandburg, "The People, Yes # 8," in *The Complete Poems of Carl Sandburg, rev. and exp.* (New York: Harcourt Brace Jovanovich, 1970), 447.

2. Callanan and Kelley, 103.

3. Kübler-Ross, "On Life after Death", 15.

4. Kübler-Ross, *On Death and Dying,* 167.

Afterword

1. *The American Heritage Dictionary of the English Language: New College Edition* (Boston: Houghton Mifflin, 1980), 1541, S.V. *Memory.*

2. Molly Fumia, *Safe Passage: Words to Help the Grieving Hold Fast and Let Go* (Berkeley, Calif.: Conari, 1992), 14.

3. Thomas Attig, *How We Grieve: Relearning the World* (New York: Oxford University Press, 1996), 201.

bibliography

Almond, Gabriel A., and Sidney Verba. *The Civic Culture: Political Attitudes and Democracy in Five Nations, an Analytic Study.* Boston: Little, Brown, 1965.

American Heritage Dictionary of the English Language: New College Edition. Edited by William Morris. Boston: Houghton Mifflin, 1980.

Arendt, Hannah. *The Human Condition.* Chicago: University of Chicago Press, 1958.

Attig, Thomas. *How We Grieve: Relearning the World.* New York: Oxford University Press, 1996.

Black Elk. *The Sacred Pipe: Black Elk's Account of the Seven Rites of the Oglala Sioux.* Recorded and edited by Joseph Epes Brown. Norman, Okla.: University of Oklahoma Press, 1953.

Bly, Robert. "Third Body," in *Loving a Woman in Two Worlds.* New York: Perennial Library, 1987.

Bonhoeffer, Dietrich. *The Cost of Discipleship.* Translated by R. H. Fuller, with some revision by Irmgard Booth. New York: Macmillan, 1959.

Borg, Marcus J. *Jesus, a New Vision: Spirit, Culture, and the Life of Discipleship.* San Francisco: Harper & Row, 1987.

Callanan, Maggie, and Patricia Kelley. *Final Gifts: Understanding the Special Awareness, Needs, and Communications of the Dying.* New York: Poseidon, 1992.

Catechism of the Catholic Church. New York: William H. Sadlier, 1994.

Cross, Milton, and David Ewen. *Encyclopedia of the Great Composers and Their Music.* Garden City, N.Y.: Doubleday, 1962.

Dent, Tory. "HIV, Mon Amour #XIX." In *HIV, Mon Amour: Poems.* Riverdale-on-Hudson, N.Y.: Sheep Meadow, 1999.

Dodge Memorial, (Ruth Anne). Available at www.iowasleadingedge.com/tourism/attractions/dodge_memorial.asp.

Ensley, Eddie. *Visions: The Soul's Path to the Sacred.* Chicago: Loyola, 2000.

A Family Thing. Santa Monica, Calif.: MGM/UA Home Video, 1995, United Artists.

Field of Dreams. Universal City, Calif.: MCA Universal Home Video, 1989.

Fumia, Molly. *Safe Passage: Words to Help the Grieving Hold Fast and Let Go.* Berkeley, Calif.: Conari, 1992.

Ghost. Hollywood, Calif.: Paramount Pictures, 1990.

Hauser, Richard J. *Moving in the Spirit: Becoming a Contemplative in Action.* New York: Paulist, 1986.

Jacobi, Jolande Székács. *The Psychology of C. G. Jung: An Introduction with Illustrations.* Translated by Ralph Manheim. New Haven, Conn.: Yale University Press, 1962.

Kübler-Ross, Elisabeth, ed. *Death: The Final Stage of Growth.* New York: Simon & Schuster, 1986.

Kübler-Ross, Elisabeth. "On Life after Death." In *On Death and Dying.* New York: Macmillan, 1991.

L'Engle, Madeleine. *Walking on Water: Reflections on Faith and Art.* Wheaton, Ill.: Harold Shaw Publishers, 1980.

The Liturgy of the Hours: According to the Roman Rite, vol. 4. New York: Catholic Book Publishing, 1975.

Milton, John. "On His Deceased Wife." In *The Top 500 Poems,* edited by William Harmon. New York: Columbia University Press, 1992.

Moody, Raymond A. *Life after Life: The Investigation of a Phenomenon—Survival of Bodily Death.* Harrisburg, Pa.: Stackpole Books, 1976.

Morse, Melvin, with Paul Perry. *Transformed by the Light: The Powerful Effect of Near-Death Experiences on People's Lives.* New York: Villard Books, 1992.

Nasr, Seyyed Hossein. *Knowledge and the Sacred.* New York: Crossroad, 1981.

Neihardt, John G. *Black Elk Speaks.* New York: MJF Books, 1996.

New American Bible. New York: Catholic Book Publishing, 1992.

Powers, William K. *Oglala Religion.* Lincoln, Neb.: University of Nebraska Press, 1977.

Progoff, Ira. *At a Journal Workshop: The Basic Text and Guide for Using the Intensive Journal Process.* New York: Dialogue House Library, 1975.

Progoff, Ira. *Jung, Synchronicity, and Human Destiny: C. G. Jung's Theory of Meaningful Coincidence.* New York: Julian, 1987.

Rinpoche, Sogyal. *The Tibetan Book of Living and Dying.* San Francisco: HarperSanFrancisco, 1992.

Sandburg, Carl. "The People, Yes # 8." In *The Complete Poems of Carl Sandburg.* New York: Harcourt Brace Jovanovich, 1970.

Shadowlands. Worcester, Pa.: Gateway Films Vision V Video, 1985, BBC.

Slater, Scott, and Alec Solomita. *Exits: Stories of Dying Moments and Parting Words.* New York: Dutton, 1980.

Sleepless in Seattle. Burbank, Calif.: Columbia Tristar Home Video, 1993.

Stolzman, William. *The Pipe and Christ.* Chamberlain, S.D.: Tipi, 1991.

Stone, Howard. *Brief Pastoral Counseling: Short-Term Approach and Strategies.* Minneapolis: Fortress, 1994.

Straight Story. Burbank, Calif.: Walt Disney Home Video, 1999.

Tarrant, John. *The Light inside the Dark: Zen, Soul, and the Spiritual Life.* New York: HarperCollins, 1998.

Teilhard de Chardin, Pierre. *The Heart of Matter.* Translated by René Hague. New York: Harcourt Brace Jovanovich, 1979.

Underhill, Evelyn. *Mixed Pasture: Twelve Essays and Addresses.* New York: Longmans, Green, and Co., 1993.

Williams, William Carlos. *The Doctor Stories.* Compiled with an introduction by Robert Coles. New York: New Directions, 1984.

Wooten-Green, Ron. "Learning Forgiveness from an AIDS Patient." *VISION,* October 1998, 19.

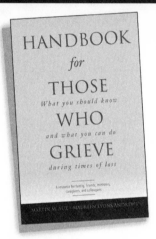